©Edu State
The Case of a Homeland State for the Nupe Nation

by Ndagi Abdullahi
(0813 798 2743 Whatsapp message only)

First Edition, September 2009

Copyright
Copyright © 2009, Ndagi Abdullahi

Contents

Preface

This book is a first of its kind, the first comprehensive argument in favour of the creation of Edu State for the Nupe people. It is the result of my active participation and experience in the affairs of the Movement for the Creation of Edu State chaired by Professor Jerry Gana assisted by people like Madam Sarah Jibrin and Alhaji Y.Y. Sani under the aegis of His Royal Highness Alhaji Dr. Yahaya Abubakar, CFR, the Etsu Nupe.

The books remonstrates that it is only through the creation of Edu State that most of the formidable problems facing the Nupe Nation today can be consummately resolve. And the book also argues that the Nupe Nation possesses all the necessary prerequisites for the effective running and maintenance of the Edu State once it is created.

Ndagi Abdullahi
Wadata Palace
Bida

The Potentials of KinNupe

I am sincerely of the personal conviction that with the creation of Edu State is the possible emergence of a fourth, actually first, unstoppable power-house in Nigeria in particular and in West Africa in general.

After so much research into the sociocultural and political potentials of the Nupe empire in the past, I have come to the realisation that with the establishment of Edu State, which will mark the official revival of the ancient Nupe empire, is the emergence of a new socio-political order in Nigeria and beyond.

If the Nupe people can hold on to the ideals of the former Nupe empire in their new Edu State, then I don't see anything that will stop us from reigning supreme over Nigeria and Africa as a whole.

KinNupe, the future Edu State, or whatever you name it, is blessed with all manners of economic, political and cultural potentials ranging from human through natural resources to geo-agricultural potentials.

We have one of the greatest human resources in the whole of Nigeria. We are among the most educated, the most industrious and the most politically active in the country. Yet all these human resources are being dissipated on the development of other states Into which the Nupe people have been segregated and balkanised.

If only we will all come together into a Nupe State then our potentials will be forged into the greatest force in Nigeria and West Africa. These are some of the issues I discussed in my book 'Nupe the Fourth Force'.[1]

My argument is that the only way forward for the Nupe Nation is the creation of an All-Nupe State for the Nupe people. Our people, the Nupes, are blessed with some of the most abundant of all resources in all aspects and facets of life, yet because we don't have a unitary geopolitical entity, in the form of a state within Nigeria, our resources, potentials and energies are wasted year in year out. It is in this context that the Learned Elders of Edu observed that, "Over the years the Nupes, despite their numerical strength, cultural dept and social cohesion, have felt profoundly marginalised and grossly underdeveloped. The huge human and material resources of the Nupe kingdoms... still lie sadly underdeveloped after decades of independence. It is our considered view that the creation of the new State will ignite a fresh energy for rapid development."[2]

Give the Nupe people an Edu State, and they will change the course of the history of Nigeria forever in a most dramatic manner positively.

The potentials of KinNupe are boundless and endless and may be said to be second to none in the whole of Nigeria. If we sit down and carefully examine every field of human endeavour in Nigeria what we are going to see is that

---

[1] In the book 'Nupe the Fourth Force' I demonstrated that the Nupe people are the First Force in Nigeria. They are the first in terms of population, political, sociocultural, and otherwise powers in Nigeria.

[2] Annexure 1, Section 1, Memorandum on the Request for the Creation of Edu State, March, 2009, pp. 21-22.

Nupencizhi record some of the highest indices in the two aspects of potentialities, that is, in terms of human and natural resources. KinNupe scores far higher than almost all other parts of Nigeria in terms of human and natural resources.

As we shall discuss in great details in the following chapters, we shall see that the human and natural resources of KinNupe are such that could build any geopolitical entity into not only the best in Nigeria but on the entire African continent.

The human resources are so overwhelming as to be incredible. Nupencizhi are some of the most highly educated people in the whole of Nigeria. Nupencizhi are also some of the most hardworking people in Nigeria. That is why Nupencizhi have the highest number of civil servants in the whole of Nigeria. In fact Nupencizhi are some of the best public service people in Nigeria. Even in the private sector the achievement of Nupencizhi are noteworthy and ranks among the best in Nigeria.

Educational Potentials

The educational potentials of Edu State are legendary. There is no any other place or region in the whole of Northern Nigeria where we see a greater concentration of highly educated people as we see in KinNupe which of course is the Edu State of the future. Have anybody ever noticed that the highest concentration of intellectuals - both academic and literary - in Northern Nigeria is to be found only in KinNupe bestriding both sides of the River Niger?

What we have here is that the Nupe people are the most highly educated and most educationally qualified and certificated in the whole of Northern Nigeria. It is no coincidence therefore, and as we shall discuss in the following chapter, that KinNupe, the forthcoming Edu State, is the literary and academic headquarters of the whole of Northern Nigeria.

The educational resources and potentials with which KinNupe is blessed are such that there is no doubt that with the coming into existence of Edu State the Nupe Nation will be transformed into the educational, literary and academic powerhouse of the entire West African sub-region on the African continent.

Edu State is already blessed with all the prerequisite educational excellence to launch it into the enviable and outmatching status of the most educationally advanced state in the whole of Nigeria the moment the state is created.

Right now KinNupe beats and outperform every other region or zone in the whole of Northern Nigeria in terms of educational and academic indices.

Despite our being termed 'educationally disadvantaged' catchment area, KinNupe produces the largest number of students of all the other ethnic groups and states in Northern Nigeria every year.

The school enrolment, from primary through secondary to tertiary, indices of Nupencizhi exceed that of any other ethnic group throughout the length and breadth of Northern Nigeria. And the same equally applies to the number of students who sit for the WAEC, NECO, and JAMB school-leaving and matriculation examinations. As a matter of fact JAMB has been consistently publishing these statistical evidences, on an annual basis, in the national dailies for a number of years now.

Interestingly enough almost all the universities in Northern Nigeria are either dominated by a majority Nupe student population or are straddled with a significant Nupe student community. Northern universities including ABU Zaria, Usmanu dan Fodiyo University Sokoto, University of Maiduguri, FUT Minna, IBB University Lapai, etc, etc have dominant Nupe student populations. While universities, including BUK Kano, University of Jos, etc, etc, have significant Nupe student populations.

With all these, the number of Nupe student graduates every year exceeds that of any other ethnicity or tribe in Northern Nigeria.

History, KinNupe and Western Education

The point here is that Western educational enrolment has been a tradition among Nupencizhi ever since the advent of the White man and Western education in Nigeria.

We also have to mark the fact that historically KinNupe might as well be among the first regions in Nigeria to wholeheartedly embrace Western education. KinNupe is definitely the first Western educated region in the whole of Northern Nigeria. Historical documentaries categorically record the fact that KinNupe was the first region in the entire Northern Nigeria where Western education was first established.

Some of the first missionary schools in the whole of Nigeria were actually established in KinNupe. And in fact the first printing press in Nigeria was established at Tsonga in KinNupe.

To all these should also be added the Western education-friendly attitude of the various Etsu Nupes in the past history of Nigeria. Etsu Muhammadu Ndayako, popularly known as Etsu Bakudu, was most especially a Western education reformist in the recent history of KinNupe. He effected the proliferation of Western education schools throughout KinNupe and ensured the unprecedented and unparalleled enrolment of Nupencizhi in Western education schools.

Such was the Western education friendly attitude of Etsu Bakudu that he even encouraged the founding and establishment of girls-only Western education schools in those days when girls are not allowed to attend Western education schools in practically every other parts of Nigeria. It is as a result of that that today KinNupe has some of the highest number of Western educated elderly women in the whole of Nigeria.

With this type of historical precedence in terms of contact with Western education enrolment and development it is no wonder that Western education has become one of the paramount mainstays of Nupe society and social values. As a matter of fact Western education has practically become a 'second culture' to the Nupe people.

Civil Service and Nupencizhi

This is what explains the fact the even during colonial and the immediate post colonial times Nupencizhi constituted the number one most Western educated and, accordingly, the largest pool of civil or public service peoples in the entire Nigerian federation. Few other Nigerian people, to this very day, can measure up to the numerical strength of Nupencizhi who are engaged in the civil service sector of the Nigerian polity.

Nupencizhi have always surpassed all other Northern Nigerian people in terms of civil service qualifications and also in terms of sheer numerical strength of those involved in the civil service sector itself. The reason why Nupencizhi have always out-performed others in the civil service sector is simply because KinNupe has the largest number of civil servants in the whole of Nigeria. An accompanying reason is that KinNupe also has the largest number of Western educated people in the whole of the Northern Nigerian region.

The basis and explanation for this is that Nupencizhi have always dominated almost all other Northern Nigerian people in terms of Western educational qualifications and other educational indices. This has been the case since the era of colonialism to this very day.

Nupencizhi the Most Educated People

No any other people in Northern Nigeria go to school as much as the Nupe people do. The school enrolment indices of Nupencizhi far outstrip that of any other people in Northern Nigeria. And, as a matter of fact, if we are to go, not by percentages per population, but by the sheer number of school enrolment and Western education graduation in Nigeria we are going to see the flabbergasting fact that Nupencizhi might as well be the number one most Western-educated people in the whole of Nigeria.

And the interesting fact here is that the number of Nupencizhi enrolling into and graduating from Western education schools is actually increasing at a rather geometric manner. Despite our already unrivalled Western education tradition, more and more Nupencizhi are become more Western educated.

We now have to look at this, namely, that if KinNupe already has one of the leading Western educated population in the whole of Nigeria then the forthcoming Edu State is going to be a Western education juggernaut that is second to no any other state in Nigeria. Edu State is going to be the leading Western educated state in the whole of Nigeria.

The vast educational basis of KinNupe is going to be of immeasurable advantage in the state-building exercise of the forthcoming Edu State. With this unrivalled educational advantage Edu State is actually going to surpass every other state in Nigeria in terms of educational development which forms the foundation and basis for every other type of development in the society.

Literary Potentials

Nupencizhi indisputably dominate the literary field of Northern Nigeria. No any other ethnic or tribal group in the North have produced the number of writers, authors, poets, journalists and other literary figures that KinNupe has produced.

Alhaji Abubakar Gimba is today the leading literary figure in the whole of the North. Alhaji Yahaya S. Dangana, the Ratibi Nupe, is another renowned Nupe literary figure. Below these two is a bastion of Nupe authors and writers the like of which cannot be found among any single ethnicity anywhere else in the whole of Nigeria.

The number of Nupe authors and writers in the Minna general metropolitan area alone surpasses the number of authors and writers in entire states in different parts of Nigeria. Niger State undoubtedly has the largest number of authors and writers, Nupencizhi of course, in the whole of Northern Nigeria. And Nupencizhi have written and published the largest number of books and booklets in the whole of Northern Nigeria.

The Historical Precedent

There is also a historical precedent to this literary supremacy of the Nupe nation. The first White people, explorers and missionaries, to come into the West African hinterland repeatedly reported that KinNupe was the literary headquarters of the entire West African regions. Islamic and Arabic scholasticism flourished in its highest form in the heart of KinNupe.

To this very day the number of ancient Arabic and Islamic manuscripts and codices from KinNupe that have survived into modern times and that were archived by the colonial and immediate post-colonial authorities of Nigeria far outstrips that of any other regions and zones of Nigeria.

And the literary and scholarly supremacy of the Nupe Nation continued into the colonial and post colonial eras. KinNupe simply became the leading centre of literary excellence in the colonial and post-colonial eras. An overwhelming number of the literary heroes who have dominated the Nigerian literary horizon throughout modern historical times have been products of the Nupe Nation. These include people like Sa'adu Zungur, Alhaji Imam, Dr.

Nnamdi Azikiwe, Ben Okri, Alhaji Abubakar Gimba, Alhaji Yahaya S. Dangana, etc, etc.

Political Potentials

Despite all the vaunting pretensions of the so-called Hausa-Fulani[1] people, the truth is that the Nupe Nation has produced far more politicians of higher calibre and in higher numbers than any other ethnic or tribal group in Northern Nigeria.

Nupe Super Politicians

Take a cursory look at the politico-administrative history of Nigeria and you will readily see the names of Nupe politicians cum administrators coming up top on the list. Names including those of the late Alhaji Aliyu Makaman Nupe, Alhaji Ahman Patigi, Alhaji Ndagi Faruk, Alhaji Shehu Musa Makaman Nupe, Alhaji Suleman Takuma, Alhaji Abubakar Muye, Professor Jerry Gana, Engr. Sani Ndanusa, Mrs Sarah Jibrin, Alhaji Shaba Lafiagi, Engr. Abdulkadir Abdullahi Kure, are a few out of the innumerable number of leading Nigerian politicians and administrators who have been of pure Nupe extraction.

---

[1] 'So-called 'Hausa-Fulani' because, in my book 'Nupe the Fourth Force' we proved that a true 'Hausa-Fulani' race does not really exist. As a matter of fact neither a true Hausa race nor a true Fulani race exists in reality.

Politicians of Nupe Extractions

There are a countless other national politicians who are variously reported to be of Nupe lineages. These include people like Alhaji Bola Tinubu, the former Governor of Lagos State, Alhaji Maitama Sule Dan Masanin Kano, the Young Alhaji of Benue State, etc, etc.

Even the four most powerful generals from Niger State, two of whom are Former Presidents of the Federal Republic of Nigeria, are reputed to be of Nupe genealogical origins. We are talking about General Mamman Kontagora, Generals M.I. Wushishi, General Ibrahim Badamasi Babangida and General Abdulsalam Abubakar.

Public Service Potentials

Despite our seeming political domination by the hegemonist Hausa-Fulanis, we, the Nupes, have produced some of the best and, of course, the largest number of public servants and politicians per ethnic demography in the whole of Nigeria.

By the way it should be noted that we have one of the highest number of high-ranking administrative officers of all other Northern states in Abuja. Unknown to most of us Nupencizhi, we are among those Nigerian ethnicities that demographically dominate the administrative set-up in Abuja as far as the North is concerned.

Nupe Civil Servants Built Kaduna and the North-Central Region

Sir Ahmadu Bello impressive venture at establishing Kaduna as the regional capital of the North was made possible only by the large number of Nupe civil servants who dominated the entire public service sector of the Northern Region. As a matter of fact it was the large number of Nupe civil servants that gave the late Sardauna the impetus and ability to develop and transform the civil service sector into the most powerful arm of the Northern Regional government of his days. And the entire administrative success of the Sardauna administration derived by and large from the solid and unitary civil service organism he had behind him.

Nupe Civil Servants Built Sokoto and the North-Western Region

Civil service is a tradition among Nupencizhi. Ever since the days of the North-Western Region of Sokoto Nupencizhi have demographically dominated the public service sector of the entire north-western half of Northern Nigeria. Neither is Central Nigeria also left out of the Nupe presence in the public service sector.

The North-Western region was effectively a Nupe enclave as far as the number of civil servants was concerned. Sokoto, the capital of the North-Western Region became more or less a Nupe city due to the overwhelming presence of the Nupe civil servants. The indigenes of Sokoto were, therefore, very happy to see the overwhelming Nupe civil servants leave after the creation of Niger State in 1976.

Nupe Civil Servants Built Minna and Niger State

But the creation of Niger State was merely a carry-over of the problems that have been in the former North-Western Region of Sokoto. Niger State was immediately dominated by the overpowering number of Nupe civil servants. Minna, the capital city of the new Niger State, instantly became a Nupe town!

Niger State has effectively remained a Nupe State ever since its creation in 1976. Now other indigenes of Niger State are complaining that the Nupe people have dominated every aspect and facet of the Niger State. These other Nigerlites are now clamouring for their own individual states wherein they will not be dominated by an overwhelming number of Nupe civil servants.

Considering the fact that civil service is a family tradition among us Nupencizhi it is obvious that the forthcoming Edu State is going to be more or less a civil service state.

Private Sector Potentials

Nupencizhi also play vital and fundamental roles in the Nigerian private sector; but this is unknown to the general public and even to the generality of Nupencizhi themselves. Some of the richest businessmen and businesswomen in Nigeria are either directly Nupencizhi or are of Nupe genealogical origins. Among this list are people like Alhaji Yahaya Imam, Alhaji Chechengi, etc, etc.

History and Nupe Commercialism

Commercialism and the business spirit have been integral aspects of the Nupe psyche for millennia far back into history. The former history of Nigeria is replete with references to the commercialist and mercantilist enterprises of Nupencizhi throughout the length and breadth of ancient Nigeria.

Nupe boat merchants have been known navigating the rivers and forests of Nigeria since time immemorial. All along the River Niger Nupe women traders and male canoe-men have been known as omnipresent commercialists and merchants.

The first Black man to become a millionaire in the entire world was a Nupe man called John Ezhidio. John Ezhidio was a repatriated slave settled in Freetown Sierra Leone.

The Need for Edu State

We have discussed the potentials and resources with which KinNupe is blessed in the preceding chapter. But Nupencizhi are not benefitting from all these, and many other demographic and statistical advantages of ours, because we don't have a national state to coordinate and channel these national potentials of ours the right way. Hence the need for Edu State.

We shall discuss in further details, in the following paragraphs, the need for Nupencizhi to have Edu State.

The benefits that will accrue from the creation of Edu State are innumerable and far-reaching. For one it will attract all manners of immense political, economic and sociocultural developments into the hub of KinNupe.

The creation of Edu State will also foist a kind of imperative unity on the Nupe people who have not been used to working together, at least since the time of the balkanisation of the Nupe Nation by the colonial White men at the end of the nineteenth century.

The grassroots development of the Nupe Nation is also hinged on the creation of a Nupe State in the form of 'Edu State' or whatever name we eventually decide to christen the Nupe State.

The New Nupe Man

Edu State is an absolute necessity for the contemporary survival of the Nupe Nation and the future global renaissance of what Henry Ford would have referred to as the 'International Nupe' - the Nupencizhi who would rule the world when a United States of Africa finally comes to dominate the world with a Superpower Nigeria.[1]

I would advised Nupe intellectuals to study the case of the Jews who are now in the modern State of Israel; the Irish who are still struggling in the UK, the Tamils who are still

---

[1] Please read my book 'The International Nupe' for details on this interesting topic of Nupe domination of world affairs in the future.

fighting for identity in India and Sri Lanka, the Chechens in Russia, etc, etc to see that the greater, superior and self-confident Nupe they envision and crave for can never emerge or be a reality unless the Nupe people are united into an Edu State.

The creation of Edu State will lead to the establishment of an environment which is conducive for the emergence of a new type of Nupe Man; the New Nupe Man. This will be the future Nupe man who is free from the insidious influences of the marginalisation and sociocultural humiliation that the present Nupe Man is subjected to.

Edu State will afford the future Nupe Man all the refreshing and enlivening facilities he will need for his transformation into the most enlightened and most sophisticated of all other Nigerian people – the very opportunity and facility that we Nupencizhi are denied of today because of our lack of an enabling environment in the form of a geopolitical state of our own.

The point here is that the Nupe man of today has all the potentials and resources to become the greatest man of all others in Nigeria, yet that has not been possible because today's Nupe man is shackled by his lack of an enabling environment in the form of a geopolitical state of his own. This unfortunate state of affairs can only be arrested by the creation of Edu State which, as we stated, can afford the Nupe man the necessary enabling environment.

Infrastructural Development

The geopolitical history of Nigeria has conclusively demonstrated that the state tier of government is the most capable arm of government in effectively bringing development to the masses at the grassroots level. The geopolitical history of Nigeria has repeatedly make plain the fact that state governments have become one of the most functional tiers of government in the administrative set-up of the Nigerian polity. Remarkable and noteworthy development and administrative exercises take place at the state-government tier such that it is debatable that it is the most useful tier of government as far as the Nigerian society is concerned.

As a matter of fact some observers have actually argued that the state tier of government is the most effective in the Nigerian polity. These people claim that their argument is based on the evident fact that development at the grassroots level can only be functionally and proficiently effected through the medium of the state tier of government. It is in this regard that Uchenna Okereke observed that, "the state level of government has for long demonstrated its usefulness as the most capable of all levels of government in extending development to all nooks and crannies of Nigeria."[1]

The point is that the state government cannot exist without the prerequisiting extension of infrastructural and superstructural facilities and developments to the grassroots

---

[1] 'Nigeria: Jaded By The Politics Of State Creation?', by Uchenna Okereke, in The Nigerian Village Square, Friday, 07 November 2008.

level. This, of course, meant that grassroots development is an inevitable consequence of the establishment of a state government. The creation of a state inexorably leads to the initiation of a galaxy of grassroots development phenomenon in a cascading manner.

State Creation and Grassroots Development

It is in this regard that we should note that the creation of more and more states within the Nigerian polity has, to tell the truth, been of great benefit and advantage to the Nigerian nation. This is because the more states that are created the more state government, which are closer to the grassroots levels than the federal government, are brought to bear further and greater developments at the grassroots level. Those arguing against the proliferation of state governments usually have a hard time running around this evident fact which they usually fail to face head on.

The proliferation of state governments in the geopolitical history of Nigeria has been, from a grassroots development perspective, of great benefit and advantage to the Nigerian polity. State creation has, as a matter of fact, brought about tangible development to the Nigerian polity. Emeka Esogbue observed that, "the creation of states contrary to dissenting opinions has ushered in new dawn of growth and developments and in addition availability of social amenities in the country."[1]

---

[1] 'Creation of More States: Broad Way to Socio-economic Developments in Nigeria', by Emeka Esogbue, in Article Base

The truth of the matter is that the creation of states compulsorily brings both super-structural and infrastructural development to the particular locale that has been accord the status of a state.

Emeka Esogbue pointed out at length, and in this regard, that, "On why more States should created in the country, the impact of this is too immense to mention here but we know that States that have been created so far in the country have all become developed more than they were when situated in other States. Anyone in doubt should imagine how many state and federal universities that existed in the country when Nigeria had 12/19 States and compare with how many in existence now with 36 States. With creation of more States it is compulsory that more ministries, universities, polytechnics, airports, seaports, Banks, press centres, mosques, church headquarters, government offices, stadiums, general hospitals, International organization centres, and other institutions necessary to make State etc that come with it. These may not all exist within a day but certainly they must be seen to exist in a state no more how long it takes."[1]

Edu State and Development

The creation of Edu State will lead to the mandatory establishment and introduction of social amenities and governmental parastatals that will in turn result in unprecedented development of KinNupe. The creation of Edu

---

[1] 'Creation of More States: Broad Way to Socio-economic Developments in Nigeria', by Emeka Esogbue, in Article Base

State will necessitate the setting up of governmental and state super and infrastructures in the various cities and rural areas of KinNupe all of which will be of general benefit and advantage to Nupencizhi at the grassroots level.

The structural development consequent upon the creation of Edu State is not going to be restricted or confined to the capital city of Edu alone. As we can readily see from the experience of other states that have been recently created in Nigeria, structural development will trickle down to every nook and corner of the newly created state. Every city, town, village and even an hamlet in the future Edu State will eventually benefit from the structural development that the creation of Edu State will entail.

Emeka Esogbue wrote that, "Creation of more states has brought development economically too to the door-step of many towns and cities, many of which have been labelled capital territories. Asaba was a town very obscure within the Mid-western region, but today, the town is on the verge of joining the list of towns with international Airport status. Oghara in Delta State is another town that has also immensely benefited from state creation, with modern developmental structures."[1]

Job Opportunities

If the generality of the Nupe people, the Nupe masses, are to effectually benefit from the democratic proceeds of the

---

[1] 'Still On The Need For State Creation In Nigeria', by Emeka Esogbue, in Articles Base, Feb 25th, 2009.

Nigerian polity then the creation of a Nupe State is an inevitable imperative. This is because the creation of Edu State will also open up a new and rather boundless labour market for the teeming skilled and unskilled workers within and outside KinNupe who may be interested in working in the new Edu State.

Emeka Esogbue continued that with the creation of a state, "There come into existence more job openings, people migrate into these newly created States to discover opportunities for greener pastures, which occasion leads to decongestions of major States like Lagos and Kano. Opportunities once again are almost immediately created for politicians who must jostle for political appointments and positions, secretariats are constructed. Roads are constructed; bridges are also constructed, with the governor of such state seeking to explore every available means of discovering means of revenue."[1]

Edu State Will Check Diasporeanism

The creation of Edu State will attract those Nupencizhi in Diaspora back home. Some of these Nupencizhi in Diaspora are among the most highly-skilled and professional Nupencizhi in the world. Yet they find it difficult to live at home in KinNupe because of the lack of a befitting geopolitical state structure back home here in KinNupe.

---

[1] 'Creation of More States: Broad Way to Socio-economic Developments in Nigeria', by Emeka Esogbue, in Article Base

With the creation of Edu State, these professional Nupencizhi will be able to come back home and be gainfully employed here at home. In other words the creation of Edu State will effectively check the evil trend of both brain-drain and its attendant capital-flight out of KinNupe.

The experience of state creation in other parts of Nigeria amply testifies to the reality of this situation. Emeka Esogbue observed that, "Interestingly with the creation of states in 1991, many people have freely moved down to their communities because of the level of development available to these towns."[1]

Nupe National Self Determination

It is also a testament of Nigerian history that the exercise of state creation has been one of the effective means of according the minority ethnic and tribal groups their rights within the Nigerian polity.

Dr. Femi Mimiko observed that, "As a definite political course of action, State creation crystallises in the crucible of the widespread concern for the situation of the minorities in Nigeria's emergent polity dominated as it were in 1960 by the three largest groups – Igbo, Hausa-Fulani and Yoruba. In spite of the Henry Willink Commission's 1957 Report to the contrary, the new political leadership accepted State creation as response to the agitation for minority rights protection."[2]

---

[1] 'Still On The Need For State Creation In Nigeria', by Emeka Esogbue, in Articles Base, Feb 25th, 2009.

[2] 'Before new States get created', by Dr. Femi Mimiko

The new administrative leadership of the post-Independence First Republic immediately realised that, contrary to the 1957 Report of the Wilkinson Commission, state creation is indeed an effectual means of addressing the plights of the minority groups who felt dominated by the Hausa-Yoruba-Ibo hegemonists.

In fact the more states that are created in Nigeria in accordance with the fulfilment of the statehood rights of the minority ethnic and tribal groups in Nigeria the better for the integral survival of Nigeria as a federal system.

Nation-Building

Among many other reasons, we believe our having a State of our own will enhance and facilitate our contribution to nation-building and the betterment of our own Nupe people.

These are the fundamental reasons why Nupencizhi have struggled over the several decades for the realisation of Edu State.

Edu State Will Stem Marginalisation

No matter what the Anti-Educi and the compromising Nupenci will say, the fact still remains that Nupencizhi are by and large being treated like second-class citizens here in Nigeria.

The Hausa-Yoruba-Ibo hegemonists have so conditioned the mind and sight of everybody in Nigeria that most of us are not aware of the fact that if you are not Hausa, Yoruba or Ibo you are automatically looked down upon as a second-class Nigerian. That is why most of us, especially the compromising Nupencizhi, are ashamed of our Nupe identity.

The first step to take in eradicating this sociocultural marginalisation of Nupencizhi in Nigeria is to ensure that we Nupencizhi have our own geopolitical state in this federated entity called Nigeria. Only then will we be able to redefine our identity, unite our potentials and power and then forge a way ahead for us here in Nigeria.

The history of state creation in Nigeria has consummately shown that it is an exercise that has proven to be an effective weapon against the marginalisation of minority or politically disadvantaged ethnic or tribal groups within the country.

Nupencizhi have decried the lack of unity among Nupencizhi for so long, yet few seem to have grasped the fact that without a geopolitical State forcing us into a single entity we will not be able to forge a real and functional unity among ourselves.

How can we be truly united when some of us are second class minority groups highly marginalised in Kwara state, Kogi state, the FCT and other places?

Those of us who are minority groups beside majority groups in other states have been completely divested of all sociocultural and geopolitical powers. Emeka Esogbue observed that, "As we have already experienced in the country, marginalization reigns in the country, and minority ethnic groups made to geographically squat with giant ethnic groups within the country have no voices at all. It is for this reason that most ethnic groups in the country continue to shed tears of marginalization."[1]

But then, even those of us who claimed to be the majority in Niger state are not spared the rigours and pangs of sharing a geopolitical state with powerful and influential 'minorities'.

Edu State Will Unite Nupencizhi

How can we be truly united when those of us who form the majority tribe in Niger State are being subjected to all manners of divide and rule intrigues by the anti-Nupe powers that be in the Nigerian polity?

The Nupes living separately in Niger, Kwara, Kogi and other states are so engrossed in their particular state problems that anybody who expects genuine unity among Nupencizhi across all these states is merely a dreamer.

The only solution is to bring all these Nupencizhi into a single Nupe State, Edu State, and then Nigerians, and everybody else, will see the 'Nupe Wonder' - the very phenomenon that actuated Frederick Lugard to dread Nupencizhi so much.

---

[1] 'Creation of More States: Broad Way to Socio-economic Developments in Nigeria', by Emeka Esogbue, in Article Base

The conspiracy to prevent the Greater Nupe ('Nupeko' or our 'Edu State') from waking up from its age-old slumber is being effected mainly through the balkanization and disuniting of the Nupe Nation. This disastrous and catastrophic conspiracy on the Nupe Nation can only be reversed through uniting of the Nupe people into a single Nupe Nation which you may call Ndaduma, Nupeko or Edu State.

Restoration of the Nupe Empire

The call for the Creation of Edu State is, in a sense, not a call for the creation of a new geopolitical entity. It is actually a call for the 'Restoration' of an ancient Nupe State in a modern form.

That is one thing that most Anti-Educizhi are not aware of. We are not begging or clamouring to be given something new which we have never had - something the Nupe Nation never had. No! We are simply demanding to be given back what we have always had until the colonial White men, best exemplified by Lord Lugard 'The Anti-Nupe', came and wrenched it out of our hands.

Nupencizhi have always had a geopolitical state, in the form of the Nupe Empire expressed in its various forms as the Gara, the Bini, the Ife, the AtaGara, the Kambaja, the Nupeko or Kororofa, the various pre-colonial Nupe emirates, etc, etc - until the White man came and put a vicious end to all that in with the two Battles of Bida in 1897.

Today, we Nupencizhi are demanding the restoration of the Nupe State that we have always had in the past and which the White man came and destroyed. We are saying today that history has vindicated us Nupencizhi over the White Colonialists. While the sun has forever set over the Colonial Whiteman, we Nupencizhi have survived the vicissitudes of history and are here exercising our national right to a restoration of our ancient Nupe State which the White man had taken away from us in the past.

So, Edu State is not a new thing. Edu State is simply the name with which we refer to our call for the Return of the Nupe Empire.

It is quite regrettable that though the Nupe State was the most powerful and the greatest in the past history of Nigeria, today Nupencizhi are without a State while all the people who we ruled over in the past have regained their ancient states in the form of the various 36 states in different ethnic and tribal locations, zones and regions of Nigeria.

The Hausas, the Yorubas, the Ibos, the Igala, the Jukun, the Igbira, the Tiv, the Edo-Benin; and even the Ijaw, the Kanuri; and many other Nigerian peoples all of whom have their own geopolitical states within the Nigerian federation today used to be vassal and subject people over whom we Nupencizhi ruled and exercised sovereignty in ancient times during the days of the Nupeko or Kororofa super empire.[1] Yet, and regrettably, today all these people who have been vassal

---

[1] Please read my book titled 'Nupe the Origin' for an in-depth insight into how in the past all the various peoples of Nigeria were originally vassal to the Nupe Nation of Kororofa.

and subject peoples to us have their own states while we, Nupencizhi, don't have a state of our own.

This time around we will not stop until we achieve our national right of having a Nupe State!

Defining Edu State

In the following paragraphs we wish to discuss some of the parameters that define Edu State.

The Map of Edu State

The question of the geopolitical extent of Edu State has also always bunted my conscience. I find it hard to settle down for the 'Edu State Map' currently drawn up by Edu State campaigners who only succeeded in including only pure-Nupe speaking peoples in neighbouring Middle Belt states of Nigeria.

In older times, the Nupe Empire was one almighty empire that exercised territorial sovereignty over large areas of lands extending in all directions throughout ancient Nigeria.

The Map of Ancient KinNupe

As a matter of fact, and as recent as the late 19th century, the Nupe Empire extended down to the very northern sections of today's Edo State. That is to say that the Nupe Empire, as recent as the end of the 19th century, included the territorial regions of today's Kwara, Kogi, Benue and other states right down to today's Edo State.

But that was towards of the end of the 19th century, the very days when the Nupe Empire was a dying hegemon prostrated before the all-pervading influence of the Sokoto Caliphate expansionists and the malicious machinations of the European colonialists. Long before the end of the 19th century the Nupe Empire was itself an almighty superpower, in the form of the Nupeko, Nupekoro or Kororofa Empire, which Sultan Bello, the Kano Chronicle, the earliest of the European explorers and expeditionists into the heart of the Central Sudan, and many other authorities reported to be the greatest empire that West Africa have ever witnessed.

Yes, KinNupe, in the form of the Nupeko or Kororofa[1] Empire, was the greatest empire ever to appear in the West African sub-region.

In the days of the Nupeko or Kororofa Nupe Empire of old the whole of today's Nigeria and its neighbouring countries, that is the entire area known to colonial historians as the 'Central Sudan' was more or less under the sovereignty of the Nupe people, the overlords of the Nupeko Kororofa Empire.

---

[1] 'Nupeko' and 'Kororofa' are one and the same words, but mirror-images of one another. Both of them refer to the almighty United Kingdom of Gara (Koro) and Nufa (Ifa, Ife, Nupe) kingdoms formed by Tsudi, the founder of the Nupe Empire. Please read my books 'Kororofa the Glory that was Nupe', and 'Nupe the Origin' for details on the fact that Nupeko and Kororofa are one and the same name of the Nupe Empire in ancient times.

In other words the ancient Nupe Empire of Nupeko Kororofa extended territorially over the entire areas of today's Nigeria and its neighbouring countries. The map of the ancient Nupe Empire of Nupeko Kororofa definitely included the whole of the Nigerian Middle Belt (particularly the western half of it) as its primary geopolitical territory. The map of the ancient Nupe Empire of Nupeko Kororofa then included outlaying and secondary geopolitical territories variously extending to other parts of Nigeria and the neighbouring countries.

The map of the Nupe State in ancient times was, therefore, a very extensive and very expansive one indeed.

That is why I find it difficult to sincerely settle down for the pitiably reduced map of the Nupe State that is being drawn up by the Edu State activists today. This smallish and extensively moderated map included only parts of Niger and Kwara states. Comparing this miniature map of the modern Edu State with the Middle Belt-wide and Central Sudan circumambient map of the ancient Nupe Empire of Nupeko Kororofa almost always reduce me to tears.

But the Pragmatic Reality

But then, after much thinking and soul-searching, I have come to accept the pragmatic reality on ground. The present nature of the overall Nigerian State is such that we Nupencizhi cannot get a state of our own with geopolitical territories extending beyond what our Edu State activists have been able to project as the map of the modern State of Edu.

The cartographers of the map of the modern Edu State have done an excellent job.

The Edu State cartographers have had to restrict themselves to areas that are genuinely agitating for the creation of Edu State. These areas are mainly concentrated in the KinNupe and neighbouring areas of Niger and Kwara states. As a matter of fact these areas are easily traceable to the various Nupe emirate local government areas in Niger and Kwara states. These include Bida, Agaie and Lapai Emirates in Niger State and Patigi, Lafiagi, Tsonga and Tsaragi Emirates in Kwara State. Of these, Bida is comprised of six local government areas while all other emirates are made up of only one local government area with the exception of the case of the Lafiagi, Tsonga and Tsaragi emirates that are wrongly crammed into a single local government area in Kwara State.

The Population of Edu State

In terms of population size, Edu State is far more populous than most of the states already in existence in Nigeria.

Extremely conservative population estimates (cf. An Atlas of Nigerian Languages, by Dr. Roger Blench, etc, etc), indicated that the population of the Nupe-speaking people tend to triple in a geometric manner every three decades.

The figures available are that there were, at least, some 300,000 core speakers of Nupe as a first or mother language in the mid-1950s. This number then tripled into a 1,000,000 round figure in the mid-1980s.

If, even going by this highly unreliable and seriously conservative estimate by cautious linguists on the field, it is evident that the population of the Nupe-speaking people using Nupe as a mother tongue multiplies three times in every three decades.

So, if we have 300,000 speakers in 1955 and we ended up with 900,000 or 1,000,000 speakers in 1985; the implication is that we are going to have three million people speaking Nupe as their mother-tongue as their first language another three decades later in 2015, that is, another three decades later.

But we are, all along, using HIGHLY CONSERVATIVE figures here which are far below the truth of the matter. As you all know, those people who use Nupe as their mother tongue, even here in Niger and Kwara State, form a pitiable margin of the true demography of the Nupe Nation.

The point is that whatever figure we have as that of those speaking Nupe at home as a first language should be multiplied several times by an exponential factor to give us a true picture of the population of Nupe people in existence.

The summary of what I was saying about the growth of Nupe population is that field research works indicate that there were some 1,000,000 general speakers of the Nupe language in the 1950s.

Since the number of Nupe speakers tend to triple every three decades, the 1 million speakers will become 3 million speakers in the 1980s and this will become 10 million in the 2010s.

We are safely around that figure now since even the Nigerian census figures indicate that there are possibly anything between 5 to 10 mother-tongue speakers of Nupe language in this first decade of the new millennium.

But, field research and census figures ALWAYS fall far short of true population figures. And this is more so the case with Nupencizhi many of whom are ashamed of being identified as Nupe. This way more than half the population of Nupencizhi in Diaspora outside KinNupe have been lost to other tribes.

To provide a margin for this colossal population of Nupencizhi lost in Diaspora it is therefore necessary to multiply the figures we have at hand by other factors. We decided, after considering many factors, to multiply it by a factor of 3 and this tripled the 10 million of the 2010s to 30 million which we projected may be the population of Nupencizhi by 2015.

The Official Language of Ndaduma

The realisation of Edu State will, by the way, accord the Nupe Nation an opportunity at the revival of the Nupe language – something that is long overdue. The revival of Nupe as the official language of KinNupe will go a long way in enabling the restoration of the historically rich sociocultural values of the Nupe Empire of old.

Part of the reason that led to the fall and collapse of the Nupe Nation of old is the imposition of foreign languages, in the form of Hausa, English, etc, etc, on the Nupe people.

With the creation of Edu State the steps can be set in motion for the sociocultural revival of the Nupe language as the national language of the Nupe Nation.

Of course, reviving the Nupe language as the national language of the Nupe Nation does not preclude the fact that English remains the official language of the Edu State considering the fact that English is constitutionally the official language of Nigeria.

But Nupe can readily be adopted by the Edu State House of Assembly as the second official language of Edu State. There are serious and fundamental sociocultural benefits to be derived from adopting Nupe as an official language of the Nupe Nation under the aegis of the forthcoming Edu State.

First and foremost the adoption of a common mother language as an official language immediately will stem the tide of discrimination and marginalisation within the forthcoming Edu State. It will unite the citizens of Edu State into a single people.

Emeka Esogbue noted that, "Linguistics should also form the basis of creating States in any environment because it is a natural cause that unity, peace and progress only prevails in an environment where the people see themselves as one."[1]

We should take cue from the case of Lagos State which adopted Yoruba as the second official language of Lagos State. The adoption of Yoruba language as a second official language has gone a long way in inducing a sense of belonging among the various peoples of the state and it has also become effectual in reducing discrimination and marginalisation within the state.

Emeka Esogbue wrote that, "The importance of Statehood forming part of the country cannot be overemphasized, it is a result of this development that the Law makers of Lagos State was able to successfully adopt Yoruba language as its second official language. One effect this has created is that the people of this State see one another as a people with common destiny. Discrimination again if ever it exists becomes limited, because the basis of intensely discriminating against one another becomes reduced to the barest minimum."[2]

---

[1] 'Creation of More States: Broad Way to Socio-economic Developments in Nigeria', by Emeka Esogbue, in Article Base
[2] 'Creation of More States: Broad Way to Socio-economic Developments in Nigeria', by Emeka Esogbue, in Article Base

Why Edu State Will Not Fail

In the following chapters we array a number of evidences in demonstration of the fact that Edu State is going to be a very viable state with all the potentials to grow into the leading state in the entire Nigerian federation.

Economic Viability of Edu State

The Senate President, Senator David Mark, insists that economic viability is a key factor to be considered before the granting of statehood to any of the domains agitating for a geopolitical state of their own in Nigeria today. Professor Shehu Marafa Bida pointed out that Edu State is economically viable.

With regard to economic viability, Edu State has no problem whatsoever. Edu State has the human and natural resources to sustain a solid and permanent economic base. In terms of population, manpower, natural resources, and popular demand at the grassroots level, Edu State is a completely and absolutely viable entity.

Those who allege or claim that Edu State is not economically viable are either speaking out of rank misinformation or out of sheer maliciousness.

As the venerable Professor Shehu Marafa Bida pointed out, the economic viability of Edu State is a fact that is beyond all reasonable doubts. There are innumerable factors and reasons testifying to the economic viability of Edu State. These include the fact that KinNupe, or the general area of the forthcoming Edu State, is blessed with all manners of natural, human and otherwise resources that go into the sustenance of a strong economic base.

First and foremost is the fact that the location of the Almighty River Niger right in the heart of KinNupe is of great advantage to the economic development of Edu State in the future.

Then there is also the fact that KinNupe has all along been an agriculturally fertile land and, accordingly, agriculture might as well serve as the mainstay of the economy of the future Edu State.

The Nigerian Middle Belt, and KinNupe in particular, is also blessed with a plethora of mineral resources the latent deposits of which can be exploited judiciously for an expeditious and remarkable development of the Edu State of the future.

The human resources of Edu State are even more promising. As we discussed in the chapter on the potentials of the Nupe Nation, the human resources of the Nupe Nation are such that they can be used to build and establish any geopolitical entity into a world-standard state in any part of the world.

We did demonstrate that Nupencizhi are presently the most highly educated population in the whole of Northern Nigeria. Nupencizhi also have the highest number of highly skilled graduates in the whole of the North.

The labour force of the Nupe population is such that can sustain the economic and otherwise development of any geopolitical entity anywhere in the world today. As a matter of fact the North, the Middle Belt, and to a lesser extent the South, are all directly or indirectly benefiting immensely and rather vitally from the scattered labour might of the Nupe population today.

Then, and of course, we have the public service, administrative, and political potentials to transform the future Edu State into an economic hegemon of Nigeria in the future.

Niger State, and KinNupe in particular, is identified as one of the bastion of civil service administrators in the whole of the Nigerian public service sector today. As a matter of fact Niger State, mainly in reference to its overwhelming Nupe civil service population, is known as the 'Number One Civil Service State in Nigeria'. The civil service tradition of the Nupe Nation is, in itself, an institutionalised establishment that can sustain a viable economic base for the future Edu State.

Then we shouldn't forget the fact that KinNupe has produced some of the most vibrant and agile politicians in the political history of this great country, Nigeria. Politics inherently runs in the blood of Nupencizhi and we possess the political might and will to establish a lasting economic base for the future Edu State.

In the following chapters I discuss these factors in some details.

Agricultural Potentials of Edu State

The paramount economic potential of Edu State is underpinned by the incredibly unparalleled agricultural potentials of KinNupe. Historical documentaries and modern studies categorically show that KinNupe is the leading agricultural region in the whole of Nigeria. KinNupe has always been and is still the agricultural headquarters of Nigeria.

Farming as the Historical Occupation of KinNupe

Historically Nupencizhi have always been known as an agricultural and riverine people. Being a riverine but landlocked people the two occupation of Nupencizhi since time immemorial has been farming on the land and fishing on the rivers. Of course the ancient fame of Nupencizhi as professional riverine merchantmen derives from their age-old navigation of the Niger and its tributaries as they trade their farm and fishing products along the breadth and length of the rivers that dissect and circumvent KinNupe.

The outmatching fertility of the lands of KinNupe has transformed Nupencizhi into outperforming farmers second to none in the whole of the Central Sudan. The pioneer European explorers and missionaries to arrive the West African Coast, including Mungo Park and the Lander brothers, all recorded, in utter exclamation, the fact that the farmers of KinNupe compares to none in the whole of the West African region. They also exclaimed their admiration at the fact that the abundance of farm products in KinNupe surpassed that of any other place in the entire West African region.

Since those historical times the whole of the region known today as Nigeria in particular and the whole of the Central Sudan in general have always depended on KinNupe as its food basket and breadwinner at the same time. KinNupe have been the region that fed the whole of the Central Sudan in ancient times. That is why there was always a well-maintained network of long-distance roads into and out of KinNupe in those ancient times as food merchants troupe to and fro KinNupe as they transport the abundant foodstuffs from KinNupe to feed all other parts of the Central Sudan.

Ever since those ancient days KinNupe has always been the bread basket of the entire Central Sudan, that is, the place that came to be known as Nigeria and its immediate neighbouring countries today.

The Sokoto Caliphate was, for instance, wholly dependent on the Nupe Empire for its food product and agricultural integrity. The Nupe Empire practically fed the Sokoto Caliphate through and through. And that was why the Sokoto Caliphate, especially through the medium of the Abdullahi Fodiyo dynasts in Gwandu, couldn't extricate itself from the Nupe Empire which was, with time, and most especially from the days of Etsu Masaba onward, tending towards the south and the sea more and more as the advent of the Europeans on the Atlantic Coast begun to change the balance of power between the Sokoto Caliphate and the Nupe Empire in the mid-nineteenth century.

When the catastrophic Battle of Raba took place in 1856 and destabilised the agricultural basis of the Nupe Empire the resultant effect on the Sokoto Caliphate was untold and Sultan Halilu of Gwandu had to rush down into KinNupe to settle the warring Nupe dynasts in order to arrest the agricultural crisis and stop the Sokoto Caliphate from collapsing due to its not being fed by the Nupe Empire anymore.

Modern Agricultural Potentials of KinNupe

KinNupe propitiously occupies the Niger valley trough which is blessed with the richest fertile landmass in the whole of Nigeria. It is in this regard that the Learned Elders of Edu Stated that, "The single most important resource base of the proposed State is highly fertile land resources, with tremendous potential for crops and cereals production."[1]

The colonial and post-Independence Nigerian administrators knew this also. That is why they established the Niger Dams Authority which was primarily dedicated building hydroelectric dams along the course of the Niger but was also, secondarily, concerned with exploring and promoting the agricultural potentials of the KinNupe area in particular.

---

[1] Annexure 4, Memorandum on the Request for the Creation of Edu State, March, 2009, p. 32.

The irrigational and agricultural by-activities of the Niger Dams Authorities led the Nigerian authorities into further discoveries. What the Nigerian authorities discovered is that KinNupe is the most fertile and most agriculturally productive region in the whole of Nigeria.

On both sides of the banks of the Niger stretches highly fertile and arable landmasses extending far away in both directions. Nowhere else in the whole of Nigeria is such a vast and expansive amount of fertile land available. The Nigerian authorities and research scientists also discovered that this vast stretch of arable land in KinNupe is also the most fertile in the whole of the Middle African region.[1] In other words no any other landmass is as fertile and arable as this extensive land that extends in both directions on the banks of the Niger in the heart of KinNupe.

The Learned Elders of Edu noted all these in the following words: "Through the then Niger Dams Authority, created to harness the waters of the River Niger for hydroelectricity and irrigation projects, over 300,000 hectares of arable land have become available in the Niger river basin between Jebba in Mokwa Local Government Area, and Baro in Agaie Local Government area, on the north bank of the river Niger. On the south-bank, in present Kwara State, we have an additional 200,000 hectares of excellent farm lands. ... Thus, along the extensive basin of the River Niger we have approximately 700,000 hectares of excellent agricultural land resources still

---

[1] 'Middle Africa' refers to the West Africa, Central Africa and East African sub-continental regions all combined in one.

laying fallow for centuries. Research findings have confirmed these river floodplains to be some of the best rice production areas in Africa."[1]

KinNupe the Rice Headquarters of Africa

As a matter of fact so excellent was the KinNupe area for cereals production in the whole of Nigeria that the National Cereals Research Institute moved its headquarters to Baddegi right in the heart of KinNupe.

The cereal research scientists discovered that KinNupe is the rice centre of the entire African continent. These scientists declared that the rice production potentials of KinNupe far outstrip that of any other region or zone in the whole of Africa. The economic implications of this are far-reaching.

The Learned Elders of Edu estimated the economic implications of the rice production potentials of KinNupe as follows: "Based on the current estimated yields of about 4 to 5 tons per hectare, cultivation of 700,000 hectares for rice production will generate a gross revenue of some N140 billion, based on the current price of about N40,000 per ton."[2]

Dr. Mu'azu Babangida Aliyu, the Chief Servant of Niger state, categorically observed that the rice production of KinNupe far outstrips that of Taiwan which is being currently

---

[1] Annexure 4, Memorandum on the Request for the Creation of Edu State, March, 2009, pp. 32-33.

[2] Annexure 4, section (a), Memorandum on the Request for the Creation of Edu State, March, 2009, p. 34.

rated as one of the highest producers and exporters of rice in the world.

The Learned Elders of Edu then commented that, "This is a huge potential source of revenue from just one crop for which there is a massive and growing internal demand in Nigeria. The proposed State could seriously become the rice basin of Africa with a great capacity for generating revenue from rice production and processing."[1]

The River Niger Economic Factor

I am particularly fascinated by the point to the effect that Edu State is an economic reality because even now, before its creation, Edu State is the economic powerhouse of Nigeria due, first and foremost, to the fact that it is the Nigerian homeland of the River Niger and due, in the second place, to the location of some of Nigeria's power plants in KinNupe.

Those who claim that Edu State will not be economically viable are overlooking a lot things and factors.

Have they forgotten that the almighty River Niger beckons us, Nupencizhi or Educizhi (whichever you call us), with the possibility of becoming the energy, agricultural, transportation and riverine commercial powerhouse of the whole of Nigeria?

With the bridge across the Niger in the Patigi area completed, with the Niger dredged to Baro, with refineries

---

[1] Annexure 4, section (a), Memorandum on the Request for the Creation of Edu State, March, 2009, p. 34.

steaming away at the Baro industrial layout, with two or three more hydroelectric dams constructed on the Niger in the heart of Edu State, with the Tsonga mechanised farms of the White Zimbabweans being the largest in West Africa, with the Americans who are already coming to establish the largest tourist site in the whole of Nigeria around the Bida general area, with so many more, ... Edu State will dominate and rule Nigeria economically and financially.

And all these industrial promises and realities are anchored on the central significance of the River Niger as a industrialising factor in the heart of KinNupe.

The Industrial Potentials of the River Niger

Whenever the issue of the economic, industrial or agricultural development of KinNupe comes up I think the first thing that should come to our mind is the fact that at the very heart of KinNupe is located the Almighty River Niger known in Nupe language as Ndaduma.

River Niger, or Ndaduma, forms the premise upon which all discussions on the economic, industrial and agricultural development of KinNupe should be anchored. I am not talking about Ndaduma State here; I am talking about the River Niger which is known as Ndaduma in our local Nupe parlance.

The River Niger defines and holds the keys to the economic, industrial and agricultural development of KinNupe. In other words economic, industrial and agricultural development strategies peculiar to the riverine dominance of

KinNupe by the River Niger is the best way forward for the Nupe Nation.

Economically we can see that the River Niger, the second largest river in Africa, is of paramount economic importance to almost all the countries of West Africa. With KinNupe occupying the Middle Niger position of the River Niger we, Nupencizhi, hold the reins of economic and political powers over the Niger not only in Nigeria but, by extension, over other neighbouring countries. Though we have never known or appreciated this.

The recent fervency over the dredging of the River Niger by the Nigerian federal authorities for the economic development of the FCT and Nigeria in general have, for instance, driven home the fact that the River Niger holds the key to the economic development of the whole of Nigeria - just the same way it had done for millennia throughout history and prehistory.

Imagine, the very further economic and infrastructural development of the FCT and many other states in Nigeria is hinged on the dredging of the River Niger right in the heart of KinNupe!

The River Niger holds the alluring prospect of fostering an Economic-Industrial complex along its banks and numerous tributaries throughout the length and breadth of KinNupe. I am talking of the development of industrial, commercial, transport and communication megalopolises extending along the banks of the River Niger in a future Edu

State much the same way that we have industrialised mega-cities clustering the banks and tributaries of the Danube River extending the length of continental Europe.

What the Danube River has done for Europe, that is, fostering the economic and industrial development of several European countries, the River Niger can do for KinNupe even much more.

Many hydroelectric dams and projects, various mechanised farming complexes, a multi-billion Naira transportation and communication network, etc, etc, are a few of the innumerable promises that the River Niger holds for the development of our dear Edu State.

Petroleum and Gas Potentials of Edu State

Scientists are now busy exploring the petroleum and gas deposits of KinNupe. The amazing discovery is that KinNupe is blessed with the greatest and largest deposit of petroleum and gas in the whole of the West African region –if not the whole of the African continent.

The scientists refer to what they christened 'Middle Niger Basin' or the 'Bida Basin' as potentially the largest deposit of oil reserve in the whole of Africa. Geographers are busy elaborating how the Niger Delta and all other oil reserves that are in all parts of Nigeria actually derives from the Bida Basin or Middle Niger Basin super oil deposits of KinNupe.

Right from along the Niger-Benue Confluence westward into the heart of modern KinNupe, the Nigerian Middle Niger area, is a stupendous deposit of fossil fuel which forms the fountainhead from which all the other oil deposits of Nigeria derive their source. In other words, and as is rightly pointed out by the scientists, all the oil deposits of Nigeria originated from KinNupe where the largest oil deposit of oil exists.

This is, indeed, the fossil fuel version of the Nupe the Origin theory!

KinNupe is sitting atop the largest oil and gas deposit in the whole of West Africa and possibly the entire African continent and Edu State is definitely coming to inherit and administer this unbelievable reserve of world wealth.

The petroleum and gas promises of Edu State are such that if well administered by the future rulers of the forthcoming Edu State, Edu State might as well become the richest and most powerful state in the whole of Nigeria.

The Factorial Problems of Edu

There are a variety of challenges and problems besetting the bid for the creation of Edu State. And unless these challenges are identified and addressed the bid for the creation of Edu State may as well remain a plan in the pipeline. It is in this regard that we have decided to identify and discuss each of these challenges and problems of the bid for the creation of Edu State in detail in this present chapter.

The Ndaduma Factor

The present Edu State Movement functions in the shadows of its much more universal Ndaduma Development Association. As a matter of fact the Edu State Movement is a relatively recent movement created by the Ndaduma Development Association. The Edu State Movement is the brainchild of Ndaduma Development Association.

Edu State and Ndaduma Movement

The point that should be delineated at this juncture, however, is that while Ndaduma Development Association is a general and universal sociocultural movement, the Edu State Movement is more or less a geopolitical or wholly political movement. This is may be compared to the case of the Zionist Movement and the Israeli State Movement. Zionism is a general sociocultural movement for the promotion of Jewish culture in general while the Israeli State

Movement is mainly a political movement centred only on the maintenance of the integrity of the modern State of Israel.

But while the Edu State Movement has gained rapid and unprecedented popularity among Nupencizhi and non-Nupencizhi alike, it is still hunted by the unpopular shadow of Ndaduma. Because the Edu State Movement is a relatively recent movement few people have anything against the new movement. But the Ndaduma movement that has been around for several decades have acquired for itself a rather sour reputation over the time.

The problems of Ndaduma are a legion and if they are not addressed and corrected Ndaduma might as well drag the Edu State Movement down with its, Ndaduma's, plethora of infamous problems and shortcomings.

Ndaduma was Bidacentric

The first problem of Ndaduma was its Bidacentric leanings. Right at the beginning of the Ndaduma Movement others have always detected a Bidacentric flair to the Ndaduma affair. The Ndaduma Movement was always dominated by a cliché of Bida elites who always wanted to use Ndaduma to their Bida advantage.

Right from the outset Patigicizhi, Agaiecizhi, Lapaicizhi, Lafiagicizhi, Tsongacizhi and all other non-Bidaci Nupencizhi immediately saw that the Ndaduma Movement was more or less a cover-up for a grand Bida plan to geopolitically dominate all other Nupencizhi through the establishment of a Nupe State completely under the control and dictates of Bidacizhi.

And almost immediately all other Nupencizhi left Bidacizhi alone in their mischievous manipulations of the Ndaduma Movement into a Bidacentric affair.

Ndaduma and the Niger State Botch

Many people are today not aware of the fact that the location of the capital of Niger State at Minna was mainly due to this same Bidacentric manipulation of the Ndaduma Movement in former times. It was the Ndaduma Movement that fought for the establishment of Niger State in the 1970s. In those days Nupencizhi were tired of being jostled around the country in building regions and states for other peoples. As the leading and majority civil servants in the whole of Northern Nigeria, Nupencizhi were first used to build Kaduna and then later to build Sokoto. Eventually Nupencizhi began to clamour for the creation of their own state in the form of a 'Niger State'.

'Niger State' was supposed to be an All-Nupe state much like the Edu State that we are today fighting for. It was supposed to be a state dominated by Nupencizhi in all aspects and facets despite having other minority tribes and ethnic groups as *bona fide* members of the State. Since in the entire region earmarked to be the Niger State of the future Nupencizhi were the only highly educated and sophisticated people in those days there was not the danger of a backlash of activism from other tribes and ethnicities of the then forthcoming Niger State.

Ndaduma Development Association was the forum effectively used by the Nupe civil servants in Sokoto State to fight for the creation of Niger State, a state for the Nupe people. The fight for Niger State was smooth sailing for the Ndaduma activists and soon the federal government responded by agreeing to form Niger State for the Nupe people. That was when a split among the rank and files of the Ndaduma activists derailed the entire 'Niger State' venture from a Nupe vantage point: the Ndaduma Movement was hijacked by the Bida elite!

It was at the eleventh hour that other Nupencizhi discovered that the Ndaduma Movement was, all along, more or less a Bida elitist affair. The Bidacentric plot of the Bida elite in their manipulation of the Ndaduma Movement in those days so annoyed other Nupencizhi that they frustrated the efforts of the Bida elite at locating the capital of Niger State at Bida which was the ideal and most fitting city for the location of the capital city of the newly created Niger State.

Denying the Bida elite the location of the capital city of Niger State at Bida was the other Nupencizhi's way of getting back at the Bidacentric Bida elites who took everybody for ride during the fight for the creation of Niger State which was supposed to be a Nupe State.

Bidacentrism disunited the Ndaduma activists who fought for the creation of Niger State in the 1960s and '70s.

The unfortunate result of this is a legacy that we Nupencizhi live with to this very day – the location of the capital city of the Niger State that Nupencizhi fought for outside the confines of KinNupe proper in Minna.

The location of the capital of Niger State at Minna outside KinNupe proper was a deathblow to Nupe nationalism in the 1970s and it almost prostrated and crippled the Ndaduma Movement out of existence. Moreover all others, except the mischievous Bida elites, left the Ndaduma Movement. Ever since then the Ndaduma Movement became more or less a Bida only affair.

Shehu Musa and Ndaduma Resurrection

So, when the Ndaduma activists renewed their bid for the creation a pure-Nupe state out of Niger state in the 1980s nobody outside Bida took them serious. All other Nupencizhi were afraid of the re-enacting of the unfortunate performance of the Ndadumites during their fight for the creation of Niger State from Sokoto.

The true resurrection of the Ndaduma Development Association came about in the early 1990s when the late Alhaji Shehu Ahmadu Musa, the Makaman Nupe, joined the movement and decided to use his superpowers to genuinely bring Nupencizhi from all parts of KinNupe together. Shehu Musa actually brought a new dimension into the Ndaduma Movement by his maintaining that that Ndaduma Movement is not for the creation of a Nupe State. He insisted that the

Ndaduma Movement should address the general sociocultural problems of the Nupe Nation instead of its being focussed solely on the creation of a Nupe state.

In his characteristic 'Mr. Fix' manner, Shehu Musa was out to reorganise the Ndaduma Movement into a general sociocultural and not a solely geopolitical movement. He pointed out that there so many other things that the Ndaduma Movement could do for the Nupe Nation apart from the recurrent fight for the creation of a Nupe state. He also pointed out that with the focus of the Ndaduma Movement on the general grassroots development of the whole of KinNupe other Nupencizhi, non-Bidacizhi, will flock back to the movement as they will see that it is no more a Bidacentric affair.

The Kogi Factor

The Nupe people in Kogi State, mostly in the form of the Kakanda and Bassa Nge people, are also the victims of alleged marginalisation and oppression in the hands of the majority tribal groups in the State.

Whether these allegations of marginalisation are true or not is not the subject of our discussions in this present work. What is our point of concern here is that our Kakanda, Bassa Nge, and other kith and kins in Kogi State need to be aligned together with the rest of the Nupe Nation in an All-Nupe State.

There is no denying the fact that, marginalisation or no marginalisation, our Nupe relations in the form of the Kakanda, Bassa Nge and others in Kogi State will be better off in an All-Nupe State rather than in a Kogi State where they share all they have or can from their non-Nupe compatriots.

The solution is, still yet, the creation of Edu State wherein all these Nupe peoples will be brought together into a Homeland that is wholly Nupe.

The Kwara Factor

Our Nupe people in Kwara state are being subjected to all manners of marginalisation and indignities simply because they technically constituted a minority in the state.

The way and manner in which various political dispensations and governments of Kwara State have handled the plight of the Nupe people of Kwara North leaves nothing to write home about.

Even the recent arrival of the White Zimbabwean farmers on Nupe soil in Kwara State is undertoned by a grisly tale of political marginalisation and manipulations.

All these go to make the call for the creation of Edu State a much more imperative one.

The late Professor Idris from Patigi made it very clear that it was Lord Lugard the 'Anti-Nupe' who deliberately initiated the conspiracy of balkanising the Nupe Nation into various states in order to break the Eternal Power of the Nupe Nation.

The Lapai Factor

The Lapai factor is a most intricate and rather complicated one as far as the Ndaduma phenomenon is concerned. It is indeed a long story if we try to take a close look at it.

A historical look at the Lapai factor will show us that since the immediate post-Independence days Lapai has been on the rise in terms of public service and political developments. It has never lacked prominent civil servants and very influential politicians. It is Lapai that produced public service and private service juggernauts of the likes of Mamman Vatsa, General Ayuba, Ambassador Ebo, Alhaji Abdullahi Kure, Engineer A.A. Kure, Alhaji Abubakar Magaji, Alhaji Abubakar Gimba, and an endless host of many others.

Lapai therefore boasts of a record list of Nupe national leaders many all of whom have contributed immeasurably to the overall development of the Nupe Nation and, accordingly, cannot be overlooked or relegated to the background. And, it is in this regard that the Lapai Emirate and its Local Government Area cannot be relegated to the background or overlooked either. Lapai is a force to be reckoned with in anything important that has to do with the overall fate of KinNupe.

It is on this note that the Lapai elite has always rated themselves as equal or even superior to the only other politically influential and public sector prominent people in

KinNupe, namely, the Bida people. This has created a silent, or cold war, rivalry between the Lapai and Bida people in general and the Lapai and Bida elite in particular.

Lapai and Ndaduma

So, when the Ndaduma Movement came up and it was initiated and dominated by the Bida elite it was quite natural and very predictable that the Lapai elite will not be keen about it.

When a Bida-dominated Ndaduma Movement came up the Lapai people naturally and rightly saw the movement as more or less an opportunity, or, worse still, a conspiracy, on the part of the ever power-mongering Bida elite to dominate KinNupe in general and Lapai in particular. The Lapai elite saw the Ndaduma Movement as a plot by the Bida elite to dominate everybody in the KinNupe of the future.

Unfortunately enough the fears or premonitions of the Lapai elites regarding the Ndaduma Movement in those initial days were, to some extent, very true: the Bida elite actually saw a future Ndaduma State as an opportunity to dominate the entire KinNupe of the future.

The truth of the matter is that at the beginning the Ndaduma Movement was dominated by people with Bidacentric persuasions, the very people who form the core of the Bida elite. At the beginning the Ndaduma Movement was actually dominated by the Bida elite who felt that the

Ndaduma Movement is an opportunity for them to dominate the rest of the Nupe people.

The problem is that it was more or less a matter of the fact that an overwhelming majority of those who initiated the Ndaduma Movement were actually members of the Bida elite. The Bida elite in this context not necessarily being Bida residents or even people of Bida origin but those whose citizenship falls within the territorial confines of the modern Bida Emirate Council. Accordingly the Bida elite saw the creation of Ndaduma as an opportunity for them to dominate and exercise sovereignty over other Nupencizhi.

As a matter of fact it was not the Lapai people alone but many other Nupencizhi who actually saw through the intention of the Bida elite at using the Ndaduma Movement to establish their dominance over other Nupencizhi once the projected Ndaduma State is created. That was why in the beginning the Ndaduma Movement received little, if any, support from other Nupencizhi apart from Bidacizhi and its elitist upper class.

Other Nupencizhi were not keen or happy about the Ndaduma Movement because they saw it right away as an opportunity for the Bida elite to dominate them. All along, and throughout the history of Nupe, ever since those Usman Zaki days, the people of Bida have been claiming supremacy and superiority over other Nupencizhi. And this Ndaduma Movement was evidently an opportunity for the Bida people to further their claims of supremacy and superiority.

But Lapai people have been a power to reckon with in KinNupe and they see themselves as rivals to Bida people as far KinNupe is concerned. So when this issue of the Ndaduma Movement came up and, instead of the Lapai people, it was the Bida people who initiated it and embraced it with all seriousness, the Lapai elite simply saw in the Ndaduma Movement another implement of rivalry between them and the Bida elite.

The Lapai elite saw the Ndaduma Movement as being a more or less Bida elitist affair which they will, accordingly, not support or promote. They felt that supporting the Ndaduma Movement will only lead to the creation of an Edu State wherein the Bida elite will dominate everybody else.

It is quite unfortunate that when the Ndaduma Movement started it was truly dominated by the Bida elite. And, to make matters worse, the Bida elite dominating the Ndaduma Movement at the beginning actually conducted their activities in a manner that will leave nobody in doubt that the Ndaduma Movement was a Bidacentric affair. This is the complexity surrounding the Lapai Factor in the Ndaduma Phenomenon.

But Ndaduma is no more Bidacentric

But I think the Ndaduma Movement needs to outgrow the selfish and traditional interests of both Bidacizhi and Lapaicizhi vis-a-vis their traditional rivalry and its negative effect on the Ndaduma Movement. We also need to work out a popular way of resolving this problem; a popular way that will not pander to the conspiratorial interests of either the Bida or the Lapai elite who are mostly the ones fuelling this unfortunate Bida-Lapai rivalry.

First and foremost we need to divest the Ndaduma Movement of the selfish interest of the Bida elite who are actually hell-bent on using the Ndaduma Movement to achieve their personal and elitist interests. Those Bidacentric leaders in the Ndaduma Movement need to be persuaded or dissuaded from perpetrating their Bidacentric ideologies. These same people should be made to realise that the Ndaduma Movement cannot be a Bida affair alone if it is ever to succeed.

These Bidacentric leaders should be made to realise the fact that with the eventual creation of the Edu State every Edu citizen, regardless of whether he is a Bidaci or not, will have equal right in that new dispensation. Edu State is going to belong to all the citizens of Edu State and it is not going to be a Bida affair alone.

Then, and on the other hand, the Lapai people need to be informed that it is actually impossible for Ndaduma to become a wholly Bida affair after the creation of Edu State.

The only unfortunate thing that can happen is what has happened in the past, namely, that the Ndaduma Movement can be dominated by the Bida elite. But this has changed. As a matter of fact the Ndaduma Movement is already assuming such popular dimensions such that it is no more an entity dominated alone by the Bida elites.

The Ndaduma Movement is no more dominated by Bidacizhi alone. Almost everybody in KinNupe is now joining the bandwagon of the Ndaduma Movement – it is no more a Bida affair.

We can all see the active participation of Nupencizhi from Kwara, Kogi, Agaie, and other prominent parts of KinNupe. So, Ndaduma is no more a Bida affair alone.

This is evident even in the religious composition of the Ndaduma Movement, it has nothing to do with religion. The Muslims, the Christians and the Traditional religionists are all actively involved in the Ndaduma Movement without anybody claiming that the Movement belongs solely to his or her particular religion.

This fact needs to be driven home to the Lapai people, namely, that the Ndaduma Movement has actually evolved beyond the stage of its being dominated by a particular set of people.

As a matter of fact if the Lapai people are to be fair to themselves and to everybody else they can clearly see that the Ndaduma Movement is no more a Bida affair but is now a Movement made up of influential activists from all parts, nook and corners, of KinNupe. The Ndaduma Movement is no more a Bida affair. The Lapai people need to admit this fact to themselves and everybody else.

Lapai and Bida elitism

A closer look at this Lapai factor will reveal the fact that the Bida-Lapai rivalry is more or less an elitist affair which we shouldn't allow to infiltrate the rank and files of the Ndaduma Movement.

Our Bida and Lapai leaders are trying to read their selfish and personal interests or rivalry into the Ndaduma Movement which is supposed to be a Movement that should have nothing to do with the personal selfishness of the Nupe elites who are at war with one another.

This is more or less a matter of our leaders taking political advantage of the Ndaduma Movement for their own personal and selfish interests. This shouldn't be the case and the masses and the generality of Nupencizhi should not support those Bida or Lapai elites who are trying to turn the Ndaduma Movement into a political tool for their own personal interests.

The masses should know that any clash of interests between the Bida and the Lapai elites should have nothing to do with the Ndaduma Movement or even with the creation of the Edu State.

Edu State Movement

Lapai people need to also know that the Edu State Movement is completely and totally different form the Ndaduma Development Association. While Ndaduma is a universal cultural movement the Edu State Movement is a political movement aimed mainly at the creation of Edu State.

Now then, one other factor I would like to raise and emphasise here is the fact that the Lapai people should know very well that Lapai is integrally located in KinNupe in such a manner that it is absolutely impossible for the Edu State to be created without Lapai being part of it.

The Lapai Embrace of Edu State

The good news is that all the Lapai-Bida elitist rivalry that we have been discussing in the preceding chapters is now m ore or less a thing of the past; the Lapai elite and the Lapai masses in generality have of recent come to wholeheartedly accept the Edu State Movement. Lapai has joined the Edu State Movement completely and the people of Lapai are now among the most active participants in the struggle for the creation of Edu State.

Wushishi factor

The Wushishi factor is a rather complicated and involved one as far as the Ndaduma issue is concerned. If we look at the Wushishi factor very well we are going to see that it is comprised of three different components or more. The situation is such that each of these three components meshes one into the other in a rather involved manner.

The Wushishi Cultural Dilemma

The first of these components is the fact that Wushishi is a mixed society of Nupe and Hausa people. Wushishi is a mixed society in the sense that we have a Nupe and a Hausa section of the Wushishi society. But the truth is that the Nupe section of the society is the predominant one.

The historical point here is that Wushishi was originally a Nupe settlement through and through. The Hausa element of the Wushishi society is a historically recent development. And, upon that, Wushishi remains to this day a predominantly Nupe society with a Hausa veneer to it. In other words the overwhelming population of Wushishi is still Nupe but the general cultural outlook of the Wushishi society has assumed a Hausa outlook.

Hausa has become the Lingua Franca over the Wushishi society. This has given an overall Hausa cultural outlook to the Wushishi society. So, to the outsider and to the uninformed, it is as if Wushishi is actually a Hausa society. It is as if Wushishi is not essentially a Nupe society which it really is. And, because of this, some people in Wushishi, and even others outside, are of the wrong impression that Wushishi is a non-Nupe society that need not be part of the future Edu State.

The Wushishi Class Standoff

The second aspect of the Wushishi factor is even more complicated and more involved. This second aspect is centred on the divergence or difference of opinion between the commoner and the elitist sections of the Wushishi community with regard to the Edu State question.

The Wushishi commoner, the overwhelming majority of which are more or less Nupencizhi, believe that they are part and parcel of KinNupe and therefore feel that Wushishi needs to naturally be incorporated into the future Edu State. But that is the view of the Wushishi commoner. And the commoner we are speaking of here is the overwhelmingly Nupe commoner of the Wushishi society regardless of whether he is a Hausanised one or not.

But the Wushishi elite does not look at things that way. The Wushishi elite has a thoroughly Hausanised outlook. And this is even though the Wushishi elite is actually constituted, in the main, of Nupencizhi – however, Nupencizhi that have been Hausanised.

This Hausanised Nupencizhi, the Wushishi elite, see themselves as Hausa and not as Nupe and, accordingly, are not really keen about the creation of a Edu State which they feel is a Nupe affair.

The Hausa section of the Wushishi society, accordingly, does not feel that it needs to be incorporated into the Edu State of the future. As a matter of fact the Hausa section of the Wushishi society does not feel that they are part of KinNupe at all.

Now then, the commoner section of the Wushishi society constitutes the majority section. And the commoner section of the Wushishi society is more or less a Nupe population. On the other hand the elite section of the Wushishi society is more or less a Hausa population – Hausa population in the sense that the Wushishi elite actually identifies itself with Hausa social and cultural values and not necessarily that it is truly a Hausa population.

So, here we are with a divided society: the commoner, constituting the majority of the Wushishi society, still sees itself as Nupe and therefore identifies itself with KinNupe and supports the Edu State cause. On the other hand we have the elite, constituting the minority section of the Wushishi society sees itself as Hausanised and therefore does not identify with KinNupe and does not support the Edu State cause.

Wushishi Local Government Bottleneck

The third, and the most complex components of the Wushishi factor, is that of the political location of Wushishi Local Government in Niger State today. Presently Wushishi Local Government Area is part of Zone C in Niger State. Wushishi is not part of Zone A.

In Niger State politics Zone A is KinNupe and Zone C is not part of KinNupe. So, if Wushishi is officially located in Zone C the implication is that Wushishi is officially not part of KinNupe. This actually complicates the Wushishi factor vis-a-vis the Edu State issue on a very serious note.

If Wushishi is officially not part of KinNupe then it will be difficult to start recognising Wushishi as being Nupe just because of the emergence of the Edu State debate. In a political sense this a serious complication.

If Wushishi is identified with Zone C and not with Zone A then politically and officially Wushishi cannot be part of KinNupe and Wushishi is, accordingly, not going to be part of the Edu State of the future.

This political and formal problem of Wushishi in regard to KinNupe is a historical one. It begun when Niger State authorities deliberately excised Wushishi, a traditionally Nupe territory, and made it part of Zone C on the superficial claims that Wushishi is culturally and linguistically overwhelmed by Hausa social and cultural values.

Zone C is politically not part of KinNupe and adding Wushishi to Zone C was tantamount to removing Wushishi from KinNupe and handing it over to a non-KinNupe political entity. Now it is not that easy to undo this political mistake that took place a while ago in the political history of Niger State.

It is actually going to be a bit difficult to get Wushishi out of Zone C and return it to Zone A or to KinNupe proper. This is even more the case considering the fact that the present Wushishi upper class or the elite in particular look upon itself as not being pure Nupe anymore but as being more or less a Hausanised class of elites.

This is where the problem lies with regard to the political question of the Wushishi factor vis-a-vis the Edu State issue.

The point that should, however, be highlighted here is the fact that the overwhelming populace of the Wushishi Local Government are passionately in support of being part of the future Edu State. As a matter of fact Wushishi Local Government is home to some of the most passionate Edu State patriots throughout the length and breadth of KinNupe. Throughout the villages and mosques of Wushishi the local Nupe people are fervently praying for the realisation of Edu State and their being made part and parcel of that future Edu State.

But one cannot tell for real how the Wushishi debacle will come to be with regard to the Edu State question. It may end up with a referendum in the nature of a popular demand on the part of the Wushishi masses for the need for Wushishi to be made part of Edu State. And, it may not end up that way. One cannot tell for real how things will end up.

The Niger State Factor

The Niger State factor in the Edu State issue is also an interesting one. Many people are of the opinion that the creation of Edu State is going to be more or less a disadvantage to Niger State.

The feeling is that KinNupe forms the greater part of today's Niger State and that the creation of Edu State is nothing but the excising of a greater part of Niger State into the formation of another state; this, of course, it is opined, will leave Niger State a small and rather debilitated state.

It is claimed that the creation of Edu State is by and large the partitioning of Niger State into two parts, namely, a smaller Niger State part and a greater Edu State part. This is why it is said that the creation of Edu State is going to be a disadvantage to Niger State. In fact this is the general feeling everywhere. And this is why those who are benefiting from the status quo in Niger State today are not that really keen about the bid for the creation of Edu State.

These people see the creation of Edu State as a situation whereby a greater part of Niger State will go into the formation of Edu State. They see this not only as a geographical or even political problem but they also see it in terms of the natural and human resources that they see Edu State taking away from Niger State. They see a greater human population of Niger State relocating to Edu State and this they feel is going to be great disadvantage for the resultant Niger State.

Niger State can Survive without Edu State

But a closer and more critical look at the situation will readily show that things are not really going to be that bad for Niger State with the creation of Edu State as the prophets of doom are wont to claim.

The truth of the matter is that Niger State does not need Edu State to survive. No matter how small – geopolitically, demographically, and resource-wise – Niger State is going to be reduced to after the creation of Edu State, Niger State will still possess all the necessary potentials to forge ahead as a viable state in the Nigerian federation.

Looking at the alleged failure or collapse of Niger State after the creation of Edu State is a paranoia that borders on inferiority complex, namely, a false assumption that Niger State needs the natural and human resources of Edu State to survive.

Even a casual glance at the present map of Nigeria will readily show us a number of states that do not possess the potentials that a post-Edu State Niger State will possess and yet some of these states are among the most enterprising and promising states in Nigeria today.

The creation of Edu State will have minimal, if any real, undeserved effect on the Niger State of the future. The viability or failure of Niger State after the creation of Edu State is going to be a function of the state of the mind of the future leaders and authorities of Niger State – it will have nothing to do with the actual relationship between Niger State and Edu State because that future Niger State will not need Edu State for it to forge ahead as a viable state.

The Partition of Niger State

Niger State is the largest state in Nigeria today and it must be divided and broken into further states very, very soon. There is no denying this reality on the part of anybody who has investigated this matter.

Ever since the creation of a number of states in the North in 1976 including Sokoto, Niger, Kano, Gongola and Bauchi, only Niger State has remained intact without being subdivided while all its 1976 sister states have been subdivided including Sokoto, Kano, Gongola and Bauchni.

Sokoto have been subdivided into Kebbi and Zamfara. Kano have been subdivided into Kano and Jigawa. Gongola have been subdivided into Adamawa and Taraba states. While Bauchi have been subdivided into Bauchi and Gombe states. Yet Niger States have not been subdivided further ever since that 1976 that it was created together with Sokoto, Kano, Gongola and Bauchi.

Niger State has consequently remained the largest state in the entire Nigerian federation today. No any other state measures up to the 76,000 square kilometres of Niger State in the whole of Nigeria today. Yet some uninformed or selfish people are still claiming that Niger State should be left intact and undivided while so many other states that are not measuring up to the size of a local government in Niger State should be further subdivided in the current bid for the creation of more states in Nigeria.

A more graphic fact is that the geographical size of Niger State is such that it is more than the combined size of all the South-eastern states. In other words Niger State is larger than the entire Southeast zone of Nigeria. And, incredibly enough, Niger State is almost of the same size as the entire South-west region of Nigeria. That is, all the South-west, Yoruba, states of Nigeria combined almost equalled Niger State.

Whether under the present Yar'adua administration or under any future administration, no any further state can be created in any other part of Nigeria without the largest state, Niger State, being included among the list of those states out of which new states must emerge.

As a matter of fact Niger State is the number one state on the list of states to be divided into further states because it is presently the largest state in the whole of Nigeria.

The Zonal Arrangement Factor

The Nigerian system of state creation is traditionally based on a zoning system, namely, that the six geopolitical zones of Nigeria must be equally represented in any exercise of state creation by any given administration or regime.

The Problem with the Zonal Arrangement

The only problem here is that the zonal system is more or less a redundant and ineffective one as the Nigerian authorities have given no any active role whatever to the geopolitical zones. The point is that the geopolitical zones play no tangible role in the administrative or geopolitical sectors of the Nigerian polity.

Almost everything about the zonal arrangement of the Nigerian geopolitical system is inoperable and has actually resulted in a big mess ever since the introduction of the novel idea of geopolitical zones.

For instance, due to the zoning system the federal allocation that goes to the sparsely populated North is almost greater than the one that goes to the heavily populated South.

Furthermore the zoning system has led to the proliferation of unnecessary states in some zones that are already 'over-stated' while the same zoning system have led to lack of creation of state for a number of ethnicities in zones that are 'under-stated' like in the Middle Belt.

The creation of more states in a manner designed to check this imbalance will be a step in the right direction. As a matter of fact state creation is an effective way to check and correct this imbalance between the various geopolitical zones.

The imbalance in the number of states between the North and the South, which has led to the disproportionate allocation of federal resources to the two regions, can also be corrected through the creation of a checkmating number of states. Emeka Esogbue suggested, in this regard, that, "Our law makers should also see to it that both regions of the country i.e. North and south have equal number of States, so that both regions will regions will have equal number of representatives in all affairs of the State. Creation of more States will therefore usefully correct this impression."[1]

---

[1] 'Creation of More States: Broad Way to Socio-economic Developments in Nigeria', by Emeka Esogbue, in Article Base

If the zones have, at least, been assigned the role of producing presidential or otherwise political candidature in an arithmetic or mathematic precision the zonal system might have been a more relevant system of political arrangement in Nigeria.[1]

Edu State and Apa states

The problem of the zoning system as it most especially affect the Edu State Cause is that it has been singularly responsible for the non-creation of a Nupe State whenever any state creation exercise is embarked on by any administration or regime in the last couple of decades. The reason is that there is always the creation of another state in the same zone in which the Nupe State was to be created.

This time around, however, the Idoma people want the creation of their own state and, with Senator David Mark, an Idoma who is also the Senate President, the creation of an Idoma State is almost a certainty.

As a matter of fact the popularity of the call for the creation of more states under the present Yar'adua administration derives its added momentum from the fact that the Senate President, David Mark, belongs to a minority tribe, the Idoma, who sees the opportunity of his present

---

[1] 'Creation of More States: Broad Way to Socio-economic Developments in Nigeria', by Emeka Esogbue, in Article Base

office as a means of realising their dream of an All-Idoma Apa State.[1]

The only problem here is that the proposed Idoma State is to be located in the same geopolitical zone as Edu State; so, it is said, if the Idoma State, with the backing of the Senate President, becomes a reality, the creation of a Edu State will be impossible.

Because Edu State and the Apa State are located in the same geopolitical zone it is said that the creation of one automatically excludes the creation of the other. This is the unfairness in the zonal system as it affects the Edu State Cause.

The Nigerian authorities, the Political Reform Conference and the Constitutional Amendment Committee at Aso Rock need to come up with realistic and fair ways of redressing this unfairness. This is because, we Educizhi, will not relent in our call for the creation of Edu State and will not agree to the unfairness of the zonal system of state creation as it affects us negatively and in an unfair way.

The Zonal System is Un-Constitutional

The truth of the matter is that the creation of a state in geopolitical zone should not necessarily exclude the creation of another state in the same geopolitical zone as long as the creation of the latter state is also based on merit. The creation

---

[1] 'The case for New Kainji State', by Abdul Nuru Sani, in Daily Trust, Tuesday, 27 January, 2009. See also 'After the agitation what next?', by Abubakar Sadeeque Abba, in Newspage Weekly

of Apa State should not mutually exclude the creation of Edu State. After all, there is no any defining or limiting constitutional stipulations on the number of states that can be created within a given geopolitical zone at any given time or instance of state creation exercise.

Presently the various geopolitical zones are unequally possessing varying and unequal number of states and yet nobody see anything wrong with that. Emeka Esogbue observed that, "Number of States comprising geo-political zones in the country are unequal, yet the basis for arriving at which zone should posses more States is uniquely indeterminate, who can tell me the reason certain political zones of the country have as much as 7 States while many have 6 and even as low as 5. This is what creation of more States in the country will set out to correct."[1]

So, why shouldn't two, or even more, states be simultaneously created within the same geopolitical zone if the need arises as might be the case with that of the creation of Edu State and Apa state in the same geopolitical zone?

The glaring problem with the zoning system of state creation is that it has led to blatant unfairness and a misrepresentation of the rights of some minority, and even, majority ethnicities in Nigeria.

The six zones in Nigeria have blatant inequalities in everything ranging from population through mineral resources to political and economic potentialities. So, with

---

[1] 'Creation of More States: Broad Way to Socio-economic Developments in Nigeria', by Emeka Esogbue, in Article Base

this evident inequalities, why the insensible, and rather hypocritical, drive for the creation of equal number of states in each of the six zones that are each and every one unequal in terms of everything?

Edu State Capital City

I personally don't mind the name 'Nupe State', 'Edu State', or any other name. And I don't mind locating the capital at Lapai, Agaie, Patigi, Tsaragi, Doko, Kataeregi, or anywhere else.

But I wonder if my Bida townsmen will welcome the idea of making Lapai the capital of Edu or Nupe State.

You see this is one of the greatest challenges the Edu or Nupe State question is facing: the lack of unity among Nupe people especially when it comes to the issue of the location of the capital city.

I have always said that in the absence of a consensus a neutral capital city should simply be founded and established in the very centre of the Edu State map much the same way that the FCT was established and built on the central dot of the Nigerian map.

I think the question of Edu goes beyond our parochial interests best exemplified by the scramble over the location of the Capital City of Edu.

There are so many sociocultural, administrative, political, governmental and otherwise benefits and advantages that the Nupe Nation stands to gain from the creation of Edu State that we need not throw the proverbial baby out with the water by squabbling over parochial issues like that of where the Capital City should be located.

The question of the location of the Capital City of Edu is one thorny issue that is, to a great extent, responsible for the lack of unanimity among all Nupencizhi for the creation of Edu State. Nobody want the capital city to be located somewhere else apart from his or her village, town or city. And, above all, everybody - except Bidacizhi - don't want Bida to be designated the Capital City of Edu State.

I would suggest, then, that a neutral Capital City be created at the very geographical centre of the projected Edu State map - much the same way that a neutral and utterly new city of Abuja was built and constructed from the scratch for the Federal Republic of Nigeria.

The issue of the location of the capital city of Edu State is a major problem. I think it is as well a paramount or even the principal problem besieging the Edu Movement. And this has always been the major problem of the Edu Movement.

Right from the beginning of the Edu State Movement the contentious and unresolved question has always been where the capital city of Edu State should be located. Everybody wants his village, town or city to be the lucky location of the capital city of Edu. And nobody wants any other village, town or city, apart from his or her own, to be the capital city of Edu.

This has always been the problem.

The very reason why a sizeable section of the Nupe population is lukewarm towards the Ndaduma Movement is simply because the Movement have always supported the location of the capital city of Edu State in Bida. Many people felt that if the capital of Edu State is going to be located in Bida why should they, who are not Bidacizhi, waste their time supporting such a Edu State Movement that is only to the advantage of Bidacizhi.

Lapai people are opposed to the location of the capital of Edu State in Bida. And Bida people are opposed to the location of the capital of Edu State in any other place apart from Bida.

The truth is that it is not the Lapai people alone but virtually every other Nupencizhi who are not Bidacizhi that are opposed to the location of the capital of Edu in Bida. Until very recent times, few non-Bidacizhi actually agree to the location of the capital of Edu in Bida.

Bidacizhi are so keen and serious about the location of the Edu capital in Bida. This is why the Ndaduma Movement used to be mainly been restricted to Bida alone.

But if we look at the issue very well we will readily see that the reason why Bidacizhi are so keen and so serious about the Edu Movement is that, to be fair and sincere, Bida has the greatest of all credentials to be the location of the capital city of Edu State. Everybody knows this fact despite everybody's primal wish for the location of the Edu capital in their own particular village, town or city. The fact is that despite all the arguments from all other angles, Bida is the best candidate for the location of the capital of Edu.

And this very reason is why so many other Nupencizhi who are not Bidacizhi are not that keen or serious about the Edu Movement. Non-Bidacizhi feel that the location of the capital of Edu in Bida will actually give a upper hand to

Bidacizhi over all other Nupencizhi. They are accordingly opposed to the Edu Movement. This is most clearly illustrated by the attitude of the Lapai elite towards the Edu Movement.

Lapaicizhi see themselves as equal to or rivals to Bidacizhi and they are therefore mainly opposed to the Edu Movement because they felt that it is more or a less a Bida affair. They are opposed to the Edu Movement most especially because they see it as a means of transforming Bida into the capital of Edu State and hence the ascendance of Bida over Lapai and all other Nupe cities.

A Neutral Capital City

In view of the intense controversy over the location of the capital city of Edu State some people have come up with the suggestion that a neutral place, a fertile land that have not yet been settled by anybody, be chosen and developed overnight into the capital city of Edu. In other words a completely new city, as was the case with the FCT Abuja, should be built from the scratch into the new capital of Edu State.

According to this suggestion we should look at the projected map of Edu State and, using our compass and divider, locate the very equidistant centre of the future Edu State and, in this equidistant centre, locate the capital city of Edu State on a neutral, hitherto unsettled and undeveloped, land. It is should be a bushy wilderness on which a neutral capital city will be built from the very scratch.

This is a very good idea; actually a marvellous one. It is a weighty concept that cannot be easily brushed aside as such.

The Problem of a Neutral Capital City

The idea of building a neutral capital city is a good idea assuming it will be easy to execute it. But this very idea has a major flaw, namely, that it is too capital intensive most especially for a new state in the form of an Edu State.

Building a neutral and new capital city from the scratch is going to be a very expensive and very costly venture – something that will be virtually impossible for a new State to carry out. For a new state to expend its inchoate energy on the building of a new capital city from the start, the result or consequences can be well nigh catastrophic.

You can't saddle a new state with the impossible assignment off building a capital city right from the scratch. The end-result is most probably going to be the ugly story of an abandoned project of a failed capital city.

As a matter of fact in the entire history of Nigeria no state has ever embarked on such an impossible project as the building of a capital city right from the start. This is because such a project or venture will be too expensive that it will sap all the energies of such a new state and may even destroy the state.

Even the Federal Government's attempt at building a new and neutral FCT Abuja is so expensive that, after several decades into the FCT project today, the Federal Government have succeeded only in completing just one and half out of the five or six phases that were initially projected for the master-plan of the FCT.

So, if we are asking a state, just an ordinary state and not the Federal Government, to build a new capital city right from the scratch, we may as well be asking for something impossible. And we are just telling that state to go nowhere economically because almost all the economic resources and fiscal power of that state will sink into the exorbitant venture of building a capital city right from the scratch.

The Solution to a Neutral Capital City

It will be far better to simply choose a city that is already well developed as the capital city of Edu State. Such a city already has a lot of infrastructures on ground that need only to be developed further. In that case the Edu State authorities will be able to simply develop the city further. And there are many cities in KinNupe that readily fit into this description. Bida, Agaie, Lapai, Patigi, Mokwa, Lafiagi, etc, etc... each one of these cities can readily be chosen as the capital city of Edu because each of them already has some basic infrastructural facilities on ground.

There are many cities in KinNupe that can readily be transformed into the capital of Edu without the expenditure of much money. The only problem is which of these cities should be chosen.

The point here is that everybody wants his or her city to be the one to be chosen as the capital of Edu State. As we have discussed over and over again this is the problem that has fettered the Edu Movement all along.

Bida as the Capital City

By all standards Bida is still the best option out as the capital city of Edu State. If we look at all the other cities in KinNupe we will easily see that none has the infrastructural development that Bida has. So if we are picking any city apart from Bida then the Edu authorities will have to spend far more money on that city, than Bida, to build that city into the befitting capital city of Edu. This, of course, will be a waste of money that could easily be averted by picking Bida instead.

Bida the Hub of Nigerian Road Network

Another advantage of Bida as the capital city of Edu State is the fact that Bida is located right on the centre or hub of the network of roads that connect the Northern half with the Southern half of Nigeria. Take a closer look at the road network on the map of Nigeria and you will see that any car or vehicle travelling from the southern part of Nigeria to the North or vice versa will inevitably have to pass through Bida or its immediate environs.

Being the hub of the network of roads extending to all parts of Nigeria is another major economic and much more advantage of locating Bida as the capital city of Edu State.

If Bida is made the capital city of Edu State and because it is sitting on the very centre of the network of roads that connect all parts of Nigeria to one another, Bida will be transformed into a gigantic economic centre of Nigeria overnight at the very beginning of the Edu State.

Bida the Epicentre of Edu State

The interesting point here is that Bida is, incredibly enough, the geographical epicentre on the projected map of Edu State.

Bida and Minna

Some other people argue that Bida is too close to Minna the capital of Niger State and that Minna will overwhelm Bida if Bida is made the capital city of Edu. These people compare the case of the FCT Abuja's overwhelming Lapai to that of Minna overwhelming Bida.

But the truth is that the case of the FCT Abuja and Lapai cannot be seriously compared to that of Minna and Bida.

If Edu State is created and Bida is made the capital, the potentials and power that goes with Bida and the very sociocultural nature of Bida are such that Bida is actually going to grow overnight and actually become far bigger and more powerful than Minna such that Minna can never ever be an overwhelming influence on Minna. In fact it is going to be the reverse: Bida is going to become so powerful and so influential that it is going to overwhelm Minna.

The same thing will apply to Edu State and Niger State; Edu State is going to be such a powerful and very influence state that it will overwhelm Niger State.

Edu State is going to be a great centre of human activity that will make it such a great state that Niger State can never be able to exercise overbearing influence on. As a matter of fact the reverse will be the case: Edu will be such a great and powerful state that Niger State might as well end up a secondary state to Edu State.

We are actually left with two options here; it is either we transform Bida into the capital city or we go and build a neutral and new capital city in the bush. But considering the exorbitant expenditure of money that will be involve in the latter option we may just be left with the single option of building Bida into the capital city of Edu State.

The Name of the Forthcoming Nupe State

There has been some little scuffles over what the name of the future Nupe state should be. Some people are opposed to the use of the name 'Ndaduma State' and in its place they have come up with a plethora of alternative names including names like Edu State, Eduma State, Cross Niger Sate, Nupeko State, etc, etc.

I have no problem with and join no issues with these peoples opposed to the name Ndaduma. As far as I am concerned whatever name the majority of the Nupe populace agree on can be used for the future Nupe State.

But I need to clarify some issues with regard to reasons tendered by those in opposition to the name 'Ndaduma State' and those in support of the name 'Edu State'. I will also touch on some other suggested names like 'Cross-Niger State' and 'Nupe State'.

The Name 'Ndaduma'

Some people are opposed to the use of the name 'Ndaduma' as the name of the Nupe State to be created. I don't actually mind the new Nupe State bearing a name different from Ndaduma. But I think I need to clarify some points as to the meaning and origin of the name 'Ndaduma' since that is why some people are opposed to the name.

Ndaduma is not the Name of a Pagan God

Those opposed to the name are of the view that Ndaduma is the name of a pagan god worshipped by the ancient Nupes. They felt that we would be honouring a pagan god if we adopt the name 'Ndaduma' for our Nupe State.

But that is not the truth of the matter.

The claim that the name 'Ndaduma' is the name of a pagan Nupe god is a product of the stark ignorance modern Nupencizhi exhibit regarding the sociocultural heritage of ancient Nupe.

In modern times Nupencizhi don't really know the origin of the name Ndaduma and they, according to their parochial fancies, invented fictitious, and rather funny, etymologies for the name Ndaduma. One of these wrong etymologies is the claim that 'Ndaduma' is the name of a pagan River Niger god worshipped by Nupencizhi in former times.

The truth of the matter is that the name 'Ndaduma' is not the name of a pagan god. 'Ndaduma' is actually the Middle Nupe epithet for God Almighty. The Almighty God who created the whole of mankind is referred to ancient times as Ndaduma.

Ndaduma is actually a phrase or a compound word comprised of 'Nda' and Eduma'.

'Nda' means 'Creator' or 'Master' and 'Eduma' means 'Large body of Water'. So, 'Nda-Eduma' or 'Ndaduma' means 'Creator of the River Niger' and, therefore, refers to Almighty God, the Overall Creator of Mankind.

'Ndaduma' is not the name of a god, of a local fertility god, solely associated with the River Niger. Ndaduma is the ancient Nupe name for the same Almighty God that Muslims refer to as 'Allah', the Christians refer to as 'God the Father', and the Nupe Traditional religionists refer to as 'Soko'.

None of these religions, Islam, Christianity, and Nupe Traditional Religion, forbids us Nupencizhi from addressing God Almighty with our local nomenclatures. As a matter of fact both Nupe Islamic scholars and Nupe Christian clergies, to this very day, refer to God Almighty as *'Soko'* whenever they are praying in Nupe. Similarly, and curiously enough, Hausa Christians refer to God Almighty as Allah or *Ubangiji* when referring to God Almighty.

So, since Ndaduma is not a god but God Almighty, I don't see any reversion to Nupe paganism by our - Muslim or Christian - adoption of the name 'Ndaduma' for a future Nupe State.

So, if we look at it from this etymological point of view, there will be no point attacking the name 'Ndaduma'.

Ndaduma and Edu State Religion

Many people are opposed to the very name 'Ndaduma'. They said the very name 'Ndaduma' is the name of a pagan god that was worshipped by Nupencizhi in ancient times. And they feel if we are now giving the name of a pagan god to a state for Nupencizhi it will amount to Nupencizhi reverting back to the worship of a pagan god.

This claim of 'Ndaduma' being the name of a pagan god is very wrong and is not true at all. It in reality showcases the lack of an in-depth understanding of our ancient Nupe culture on the part of our Nupe elite and even the generality of Nupencizhi.

In the first place we should mark the fact that this attack against the use of the name 'Ndaduma' comes solely from among the Muslim and Christian Nupencizhi.

Muslim and Christian Nupencizhi allege that 'Ndaduma' is the name of a pagan Nupe god and that they are not ready to worship a pagan Nupe god. But then, even if we take it that way, are we not overlooking the fact that there is a sizeable population of traditional religionist, Nupencizhi among the population of Nupencizhi here in KinNupe? Or are we saying that those who are not Muslims or Christians in the future Edu State are going to be marginalised religiously?

Edu State, being a state within the Federal Republic of Nigeria, is going to be a secular state wherein everybody is free to practise the religion of his choice and, as such, the religious persuasions of the Muslim and Christian citizens of Edu State cannot be imposed on that of the traditional religionist citizens of Edu State.

If Muslim and Christian Nupencizhi are opposed to the use of the name 'Ndaduma' because they felt it is the name of a pagan god, then where is the right of the Traditionalist Nupencizhi among us? It is a fact that there is a sizeable population of traditional religionist Nupencizhi who are neither Muslims nor Christians and these people are also going to be integral citizens of the future Edu State.

The attack against the use of the name 'Ndaduma' is more or less a religious attack which is not supposed to be the case in a secular state like Edu State. If we allow this insidious attack against the Traditionalist Nupencizhi among us today simply because they are too few in number to fight back then we will be setting a vicious precedent of religious marginalisation and crises in the future Edu State.

This is the first problem associated with the attack against the use of the name 'Ndaduma' – the fact that it is more or less a religious attack.

Religious biases or religious differences are not supposed to feature in a Edu State which is supposed to be a multi-religious secular state.

And if we don't stem the tide of religious biasness right now then we are simply planting a religious time-bomb that can come and set Nupencizhi of different religious faiths against each other in the future Edu State – something that has the potential of viciously tearing a future Edu State apart.

Right now, even before the creation of Edu State, it should be clearly stated out in the Edu State Manifesto or Constitution that no religious group or denomination has the right to come and start claiming supremacy or superiority over another religion in the future Edu State.

So, looking at this issue of the name 'Ndaduma' from a religious point of view, there is no point in rejecting the name 'Ndaduma' simply because it is assumed to be the name of a pagan god.

Edu State

Some others have suggested the name 'Edu'. As a matter of fact, and with the strong lobby of a section of the Nupe elite from Kwara State, this name Edu as gained some currency as a possible name to be adopted for the forthcoming Nupe State.

There are, however, many problems and troubles associated with the adoption of the name 'Edu' as the name of the forthcoming Nupe State. I will discuss some of these below.

Edu Confuses with Edo

The first problem with this name is that it is so phonetically similar to the name 'Edo' of the Edo-Benin people of Edo State that it consequently lacks any originality at all.

And of course, on the political map of Nigeria, there will always be this unfortunate mistaking of Edu for Edo or vice versa especially by those who are not that familiar with Nupe or Nigerian polities.

Edu is Kwaran

Then Nigerlite Nupencizhi, with good reasons, pointed out that 'Edu' is the name of a local government in Kwara State and, in adopting it as the name of an entire Nupe State, we run the risk of a future rejection of the name by those who will see it as a political gimmick at imposing the name of a Patigi-Lafiagi-Tsonga-Tsaragi axis locality on the whole of the Nupe Nation. For those with in-depth knowledge of Nupe history, there are serious historico-political implications of negative knock-on effects in this.

It should be noted that Bidacizhi have passionately dreamt of naming the forthcoming Nupe State as 'Bida State' but have to bow down to reasonable opposition to the imposition of the name of a Nupe locality, Bida, on the entire Nupe Nation.

The argument, from the side of the Bida advocates, is that if Bidacizhi would not have their way in imposing the name of their beloved Bida on the forthcoming Nupe State then the people of Edu Local Government in Kwara State would have to also bow down to the reasonable opposition to the imposition of the name of their local government on the whole of the forthcoming Nupe State.

To forestall an intra-Nupe internecine clash between the Dendo dynasts, in Bida, and Tsudi dynasts, in Kwara State, in the forthcoming Nupe State it would be quite prudent right now to put aside the name 'Edu' in order to sensibly prevent the name 'Edu' from becoming a sensational source of civil crisis in the future Nupe State.

Cross-Niger State

Some other people have suggested calling the Nupe State 'Cross-Niger'. Others said it should be 'Cis-Niger' while some others have even naively said it should be called 'Trans-Niger' State.

The problem with all these 'Niger' names is, first and foremost, the fact that 'Niger' is a English word.

We have been unfortunate enough as Nigerians to have a name of English origin imposed on us by the colonial White men. And those of us in Niger State have been doubly unfortunate to have imposed on ourselves a state name of English origin. I think this is not an occasion for us Nupencizhi to repeat that eternal crime of imposing a foreign name on ourselves as if we don't have a culture of our own.

Nupe culture and the Nupe language have such an opulent vocabulary that we don't have to look up a English dictionary to pick a name for an All-Nupe State. The name for a Nupe State should be an indigenous and pure Nupe word.

Also, the name 'Cross-Niger' has a tinge of inferiority complex attached to it. When we say 'Cross-Niger State' we are subconsciously infusing an inferiority complex with regard to Niger State and Cross River State that already exist in Nigeria. It is as if Nupencizhi are now second to or are imitating Niger State or Cross Rivers State.

Nupe State

Some others have suggested the name 'Nupe State'.

Many have opposed the name 'Nupe State' on the ground that we would be naming a state after the national name of tribe if we call it Nupe State.

But the truth of the matter is that there is no any problem in naming a state after a tribe or ethnicity. After all the entire enterprise of state or nation-building is actually that of allocating a sovereign state to a tribal, ethnic or racial group in search of self-determination.

Saying that the Nupe State should not be named after a tribe is more or less the same line of argument as those who said that Edu State should not be created at all because it is a tribal state. But that is a fallacious way of thinking. We have refuted such claims in a section of this present work.

I will only like to point out here that if you look at the map of Nigeria you will easily see that so many states are actually named after tribes and ethnicities across the length and breadth of this expansive country.

Then we should also mark the fact that almost every state in Nigeria was actually carved out for a particular or group of tribes in Nigeria. There is no state in Nigeria that was not created mainly due to the agitation of a tribe or group of tribes for their own political sovereignty.

So, whether we admit it or not, state creation in Nigeria has to do with tribal or ethnic considerations. We, therefore, cannot the reject the name 'Nupe State' as the name of the future Nupe State simply because it includes the national name of the Nupe tribe or ethnicity.

Anti-Eduism

Some people are opposed to the creation of Edu State. These are the people we refer to as the 'Anti-Educizhi'. The Anti-Educizhi are not all the same; there are different types of Anti-Educizhi and the only common ground they share is that they are all opposed to the idea of the creation of a Nupe State.

Opposition to the creation of states in Nigeria is a nationwide phenomenon and is not restricted to Anti-Eduism alone. However, Anti-Eduism, being more or less a subset of the general opposition to state creation, shares a lot in common with the overall opposition to state creation in other parts of Nigeria.

The myriad of arguments tendered by the Anti-Educizhi and those opposed to state creation in general have, however, been competently refuted by relevant political scientists and experts in related fields. These professionals have demonstrated that arguments in opposition to state creation are actually baseless and unfounded. Emeka Esogbue lamented that, "It grieves me so much when I read from Nigerians that we do not need further creation of states."[1]

Anti-Edu Nupencizhi

It is rather amazing to see that there is indeed a section of the Nupe population, however a marginal one, that is

---

[1] 'Still On The Need For State Creation In Nigeria', by Emeka Esogbue, in Articles Base, Feb 25th, 2009.

opposed to the idea of the creation of Edu State. One would have thought that no Nupenci, in his right senses, would have been opposed to the idea of the creation of a Nupe State. But the fact is that there are Nupencizhi who are opposed to the idea of the creation of a Nupe State.

The problem with those Nupencizhi opposed to the creation of Edu State is that most of them are of the persuasion that the creation of Edu State is not going to be possible. They come up with all manners of silly reasons: it is going to be a very difficult venture; many people have tried it in the past and failed; the Nigerian authorities in Aso Rock are not interested in Edu State; the over-powerful or 'superpower' generals in Minna are not interested in Edu State; we Nupencizhi are already dominating Niger State, why look for another Nupe-dominated Edu State?; the proliferation of state creation is an exercise against national integration; and so on and on.

Well, let me tell you one thing: Edu State was not possible or viable in the past because its time has not come then. Now the time of Edu State has come and nothing, I repeat: nothing, can stop the actualization of Edu State now.

Have these pessimists forgotten the glaring fact that Niger State is the largest state in the whole of Nigeria today and that there is no way a new state can be created in any other part of Nigeria today without the question of the partition of Niger State into further states being settled first

Diaspora and Anti-Eduism

A common characteristic of the Anti-Edu Nupenci is that most of them are Nupencizhi in Diaspora. It is quite rare to see a Nupencizhi right in the heart of KinNupe who is genuinely opposed to the idea of a Edu State. The Anti-Educi Nupenci is almost always to be found among non-Nupe circles of Anti-Educizhi outside the confines of KinNupe proper.

On the other hand, we are not saying that all the Nupencizhi in Diaspora are Anti-Educizhi. On the contrary an overwhelming majority of the staunchest, most committed and diehard Educizhi actually comes from the fold of the Nupencizhi in Diaspora.

But those Nupencizhi who are always or mostly in the midst or circles of Anti-Educi non-Nupencizhi are usually the ones who end up as the Anti-Edu Nupencizhi. These Anti-Educi Nupencizhi are mostly found in the Minna-Abuja axis.

Compromising Nupencizhi

There is an annoying bunch of Nupencizhi whom I refer to as the 'Compromising Nupe'. These lethargic or cowardly Nupencizhi love to tell the world that they don't mind not having a Edu State for the Nupes.

While the truth of the matter is that these Compromising Nupencizhi actually wish for an Edu State secretly in their minds, they dare not voice it out due to the barrage and battery of criticisms and attacks they might receive from their peers, their friends and their masters most of whom are not Nupes.

I used to be like that before too. I used to be ashamed of and afraid of a Nupe identity before...

...But I think the time has come for Nupencizhi, especially the Compromising Nupenci, to throw away the yoke of servitude to the interest and whims of non-Nupencizhi at the cost of Nupe suffering.

The creation of Edu State is not going to come on a platter of gold for us Nupencizhi. Edu State will deserve some personal sacrifice, no matter how small, on our parts.

Anti-Edu Arguments

Those opposed to the idea of the creation of Edu State array a number of arguments in defence of their opposition. Their arguments are generally centred around a primary premise to the effect that Edu State cannot stand or survive on its own. Another, rather secondary, premise is that the creation of Edu State is more or less an unnecessary undertaking considering the fact that Nupencizhi are comfortable in the various states they have been segregated into and not really complaining about their present status quo.

There are many more arguments and lines of reasoning ranged by the Anti-Educizhi. They say Nupencizhi are not united; that KinNupe lack any economic institution or financial establishment to support the fiscal survival of an Edu State; that we, Nupencizhi, are already occupying the superior and officious positions in various states and therefore don't need any Edu State; that the creation of Edu State, an All-Nupe state, is an exercise in promotion of tribalism; that the endless exercise of state creation will only lead to a national disintegration of the of the Nigerian polity and that national integration is the goal of the Nigerian Constitution...

...The argument of the Anti-Educizhi is a legion...

But none of the arguments of the Anti-Educizhi is valid or well-founded. As a matter of fact all the arguments of the Anti-Educizhi are not defensible. In the following chapters we refute and disprove these indefensible and invalid arguments of the Anti-Educizhi.

The Alleged Incapability of Edu State

Some people argue that Edu State cannot sustain itself as a viable state.

I will start by asking that have these people forgotten that almost all the regions and states created ever since the beginning of Nigeria in 1914 all took place when those same regions and states seemed apparently not ready or not capable to sustain themselves; just the same way that Edu State seems today.

In particular I would like us to cast our minds to the instance of state creation in 1967 when Gowon, in an *ad hoc* manner, instantaneously created twelve states out of the former regions without even the prior awareness of the peoples who were overnight carved into states the responsibilities of the sustenance of which were suddenly thrown upon their shoulders? None of these states became a failed state afterwards as the Anti-Educizhi seems to be extrapolating for the Edu State.

First, I don't agree with the allegation that the projected Edu State has not the ability to sustain itself. In the first place you don't need to have a self-sustaining geopolitical zone before you create or transform it into a semi-autonomous or self-sustaining state. What you need is a regional or sub-national collection of people who are ready to live together and work together for the development and sustenance of the state they want to be created. It is after the creation of the state that the issue and question of how to sustain it through hard work, determination, good governance and all the other paraphernalia of governance and development arise.

Niger State Majority

Some Anti-Educizhi claim said that Nupencizhi have always been the powers that be in Niger State and that that is one of their reasons for not liking the very idea of Edu State.

I don't see a strong reason there.

The fact is that I have heard his argument over and over again from Anti-Educi proponents for so long that I have been forced to work out the fallibility of that claim.

Marginalised Nupe Nation

Our being the majority and the power that be in Niger State does not preclude the fact that we are still a highly marginalised nation of people in the federated system of the overall Nigerian nation. And this is due mainly to the fact that we have been demographically balkanised into puny local governments and zones in various states that cannot pay attention wholly to our national Nupe needs simply because we share all these states with others.

I would also like you to mark the fact that the balkanisation of Nupencizhi into a majority in Niger state and puny minorities in various other states have only led to a sum total of marginalisation of the entire Nupe Nation at the federal level.

Nupencizhi are being painfully under-represented at the National Assembly and at all other federal parastatals. If there were an Edu State, for instance, the number of Nupencizhi who are ministers, permanent secretaries, directors, etc, etc, at the federal level would have been far more than what it is today without an Edu State.

At the National Assembly there are only two Nupe Senators and only four or so Nupe Members of the House of Representatives. Imagine the National Assembly that has a combined population of close to a thousand members of the Upper and Lower Houses less than ten are Nupencizhi!... and this ghastly scenario derives mainly from the fact that there is not a geopolitical state for the Nupe people.

Nupencizhi cannot get what they completely want or deserved in all the states - Niger, Kwara, Kogi, FCT, etc - because we share all these states with others. We can only get our national aspirations fulfilled if we have a state that is wholly ours and which we can then administer according to our own Nupe worldview.

Marginalised Nupe Minorities

But the main issue in this context of marginalisation is the fact that Nupencizhi are found not only in Niger State but also in all the neighbouring states and the FCT.

Now then, we all know that the Nupencizhi in all these other states are minorities and are humiliatingly marginalised in all these neighbouring states. The creation of an Edu State will bring all these Nupencizhi into the fold of a single state and will put an end to the issue of the marginalisation of others by majority Nupencizhi in Niger state and the marginalisation of minority Nupencizhi by others in other states.

Claims of a Nupe-dominated Niger State, rather parenthetically, overlook the fact that our less fortunate brothers are incarcerated as powerless minorities in other states most especially including in Kwara and Kogi states. The only way to save these brothers and sisters of ours across the Niger is to establish an Edu State that will bring all of us back into a single geopolitical entity in the form of a modern Nigerian state.

Emeka Esogbue wrote that, "Creation of States should rather gather displaced peoples who see themselves as lost because they are forcefully made to stay in the midst of people who they are bound to distance themselves from. It is for this reason that agitation for State creation continues. People should not be unwillingly placed where they not belong."[1]

---

[1] 'Creation of More States: Broad Way to Socio-economic Developments in Nigeria', by Emeka Esogbue, in Article Base

Nupe Marginalisation of Other Nigerlites

Then we shouldn't also forget the fact that celebrating the claim that Nupencizhi are the majority in Niger state has its own seamy sides. If we are happy that Nupencizhi are the majority in Niger State then we are indirectly saying that we are happy that, as a majority in Niger State, we are marginalising the minority non-Nupe ethnicities and tribes in Niger State.

Nupencizhi are not marginalised in Niger state. As a matter of fact, and because Nupencizhi are the majority in Niger state, Nupencizhi are the ones who, allegedly, are wrongly marginalising others in Niger state.

The fact that Nupencizhi are not marginalised in Niger state, however, does not constitute a valid argument against the concept of an Edu State. In truth, this fact actually argues in favour of the creation of Edu State - most especially in order to stop the alleged wrongful marginalisation of the Gbagyis, the Hausa, the Kambaris, the Kamukus and others in Niger state. Marginalising others has only contributed to a stigmatisation of Nupencizhi with a bad identity in Niger state.

Nupe Is Not The Power In Niger State

However, claims of Nupe majority and Nupe domination of others in Niger State have better been treated or even discussed with caution. The uncanny truth remains that demographic or numerical supremacy does not accord the

Nupencizhi the *de facto* power in Niger State. The point is that the politically ruling elite that hold the reins of real power in Niger State are not Nupe or do not readily identify with the Nupe.

Anybody with even a casual idea of the power play in Niger State knows very well that Nupencizhi, despite their demographic supremacy, do not constitute the real powers that be in Niger State. The ruling and 'superpower' elite in Niger State do not identify with the Nupe Nation.

Edu State a Tribal State?

Some people argue in opposition to the creation of Edu State by claiming that it is going to be an ethnic or tribal state. They then point out the fact that ethnicity or tribalism is against the dictates of the Constitution of the Federal Republic of Nigeria.

The argument that the proliferation of states in Nigeria will lead to heightened tribalism and ethnic clash is a general and universal one and might not necessarily be specific to the Edu State case. Abubakar Sadeeque Abba has, for instance, argued, in a catholic manner, that, "The agitations for state creation will only further divide the various ethnic groups in the country who were known to have had mutual suspicion and mistrust of one another; thus deeping conflict and crisis among these nationalities."[1]

The truth of the matter is that this line of argument is completely and totally wrong.

---

[1] 'After the agitation what next?', by Abubakar Sadeeque Abba, in Newspage Weekly

I will start by drawing your honourable attention to the fact that Nigeria is constitutionally a federal republic with a greater slant to the federal aspect. In other words the various peoples, states and nationalities that goes into forming the Federal Republic of Nigeria are constitutionally supposed to be afford enough autonomy such as to avoid the complaint of coercion or marginalising oppression on the part of any of these various entities within the Nigerian federation. In this regard every ethnic and tribal group, including Nupencizhi, have the constitutional and even legal right to demand for their own relatively autonomous ethnic nation or state within the overall Nigerian nation.

Granting Nupencizhi their own state does not and cannot tamper with the federal, and also democratic republican nature, of Nigeria which was established right from the beginning with a provision for the establishment of ethnic or tribal considerations.

In other words there is no legal or constitutional problem with the establishment of a Nupe State within the Federal Republic of Nigeria because, as a federal republic, Nigeria came into existence with a constitution that was originally drafted and ratified for addressing this problem.

Ethnic States in Nigeria

Another factor that we must look at is that many other states within Nigeria today were founded and established based on ethnic or tribal criteria (never mind their names being christened after rivers); yet none of these states have became a source of any trouble to Nigeria whatever due to tribal or ethnic issues.

Furthermore, I would like you to know that the unity and stability of a federated system like Nigeria is more assured only through the granting of partial autonomy to very large ethnic or tribal groups of the likes of the Nupe.

Everybody is aware of the fact that Nupe is one of the largest ethnic groups in Nigeria. As a matter of fact in my book titled 'Nupe the Fourth Force', I categorically demonstrated the fact that Nupe is that largest ethnic group in Nigeria - larger than each one of the Hausa, Yoruba and Ibo groups.

Denying such a large ethnic group like the Nupes a state of their own will only amount to setting up a time-bomb which can explode and shatter the Nigerian federation apart at any time in the near future.

To ensure national unity let large ethnic groups like the Nupe and the Idoma have their own states.

Edu State and National Integration

Others have argued that, "If every tribe in Nigeria that thinks it is large enough calls for creation of their own state; don't you think we will be heading for tribal segregation rather than national integration?" I will answer as follows:

In a federal republic like Nigeria the constitutional imperative is that all major ethnic or tribal groupings must have their geopolitical interests addressed - otherwise the federal republic will cease to be a viability.

In the same regard, minority groups need to aligned or combine together in order to call out for and establish their own geopolitical entities wherein their civil and legal rights will be constitutionally ensured in such a manner that one minority group does not have the upper hand over another minority group in such a conglomerative geopolitical state of affiliated minorities...

... But Nupe is a majority ethnic phenomenon. Just the way the Hausa, Yoruba and the Ibos had the Northern, Western and Eastern Protectorates (later Regions and now Zones) geopolitically carved out respectively for each of them, other major ethnic groups in Nigeria - including the Nupe, the Tiv, the Ijaw, and others - need to have their own geopolitical states or zones carved out for them. This is a constitutional requirement or right and has nothing to do with the disintegration of a truly federated Nigeria.

As a matter of fact the strength or integrity of the unity of Nigeria lies more in the federated system where all the major - and minor - tribal or ethnic groups are dully accorded their rights through the establishment of segregated states within which they can exercise their partial sovereign or autonomous rights.

That Nupe is a majority group is beyond all doubt and all research workers are agreed on this. In my book, 'Nupe the Fourth Force', I actually proved that Nupe is demographically greater and larger than the Hausa, Yoruba and Ibo. It is quite unfortunate that this fact has been insidiously hidden from the sight of the general public. But we are now publishing the facts.

That Nupe is larger in population than the Hausa, Yoruba and Ibo is a fact that is well known among the intelligentsia ever since the days of the Colonial Government in Nigeria. That was why Lord Lugard, George Goldie and others were in eternal fear of the Nupe. They introduced the system of Indirect Rule in the Northern Protectorate because that was the only way to subjugate the Nupe.

After Independence the First Republic administration of the Northern Region headed by the Sardauna, Tafawa Balewa, Kasim Ibrahim and others were also afraid of the Eternal Nupe and did all they could to stop the shattering of the Northern Region into a Northern Region proper in North-central Nigeria and a Nupe Region comprising the whole of the Middle Belt.

It was the fear of the rise of a Nupe Region that stopped the Second Republic Northern politicians from supporting Isaac Boro and his militant Ijaw group which was fighting for the establishment of a Delta-Rivers Region in the south.

So the fact that Nupe is a majority ethnicity in Nigeria is well known in exclusive circles and Nupe, accordingly, deserve a geopolitical state of its own. The creation of a Nupe State will not lead to the disintegration of Nigeria. It will only integrate Nigeria further.

Edu State is Not Another Biafra

Others, maybe out of desperation, have gone to the extent of likening the creation of Edu State to a secessionist venture in the like of the failed Biafra of old.

One would have not wasted the time to refute the arguments of those comparing Edu to Biafra but for the fact that the layman and the uninformed will take such baseless arguments serious.

Biafra was a call for secession, that is, a call for the creation of a new sovereign nation carved out of the Federal Republic of Nigeria. But Edu is not a secessionist state; Edu is a semi-autonomous state completely subjected to the federal laws of Nigeria and under the central control of Abuja.

Nupencizhi are proud to be Nigerians. No Nupenci has ever thought or even imagined that an Edu State independent of the Federal Republic of Nigeria will ever survive or will be a feasible phenomenon on the international scene.

As a matter of fact in the *Memorandum On the Request for the Creation of Edu State* submitted by the Edu State Movement to the Nigerian National Assembly at Abuja, the Learned Elders of Edu categorically declared that their resolution to request for the creation of Edu State is a secondary premise based on their primary identification as a Nigerian people. The Nupe elders stated that, "Inspired by the strong resolve of the National Assembly to uphold the provisions of the Constitution of the Federal republic of

Nigeria; encouraged by your patriotic determination to amend Nigeria's Constitution to reflect the wishes, yearnings and aspirations of the people; and moved by the profound yearnings and strong desires of our peopled for a STATE of their own; we the leaders and representatives of the entire people of Bida, Borgu, Agaie, and Lapai Emirates of Niger State; Pategi, Lafiagi, Shonga and Tasaragi Emirates of Kwara State, hereby present our request for the creation of a new state to be known as EDU STATE."[1]

As is clear from the above quoted Section 1, Article 1, of the Memorandum for the Creation of Edu State, the Nupe people consider themselves primarily as Nigerians and they see their call for the creation of Edu State only as a secondary identity.

But the very call for Biafra begun with a premise based on the belief among the Igbo elite that an Ndi Igbo state - subsisting on the oil fields of the Ijaw, Ogoni or the general Ogoja-Rivers-Calabar area - will not only survive on its own independent of a federated Nigeria but that such a small but oil rich state will be the richest country in not only Africa but in the entire world. That was why France and Israel jumped into the blind support of Biafra during the Biafran War - they were both desperately in need of a small but super oil-rich country in Third World Africa.

So, the call for an Edu State dependent on the Federal Republic of Nigeria is completely different and actually

---

[1] Section 1, article 1, Memorandum on the Request For the Creation of Edu State, March, 2009, pp. 2-3.

opposed to a call for a secessionist state of Biafra which is completely independent of Federal Republic of Nigeria.

The Unity of Edu State

Others have argued that Nupencizhi are not united enough to be bequeathed an Edu State wherein they will only fight and clutch at one another's necks.

This argument is also unfounded and I will disprove it as follows:

It is true that the Nupe Nation is not united. There are both superficial and deep-rooted strands of disunity between the various sections, classes and levels of the Nupe Nation. There are religious, cultural, dialectal, class, royal, economic and even geophysical differences and disunities among Nupencizhi.

Historical Balkanisation

Then we should also mark the fact that there is also a historical tinge to this disunity that has hallmarked the KinNupe in recent times. To some extent the lack of unity among Nupencizhi can be blamed on external or outside factors as is applicable in the case of the colonial powers who deliberately and by premeditated design foisted a grand scheme of disunity on the Nupe Nation.

The series of political and commercial encounters between the Nupe Empire and the British Empire in the latter half of the nineteenth century eventually led to the staunch resolution on the part of the Royal Niger Company authorities to decapitate the "very large and dangerous" Nupe empire.

It was the Royal Niger Company administrative set-up that eventually became the Colonial Government of Nigeria through its obtaining of a charter from the Colonial Office of the British Empire. And it was the same head officers of the RNC who became the colonial governors of the resultant Nigeria.

People like Lord Lugard and Sir George Taubman Goldie, who headed the RNC and were personally involved, and actually headed the battles and hostilities with the Nupe Empire during the days of the RNC, became the rulers and governors of Nigeria in the days of the Colonial Government of Nigeria. These people were already inoculated with heavy doses of prejudices against the Nupe Nation and did all they could in balkanising the Nupe Empire into a decapitated collection of weakling puny states in the form of powerless emirates and kingdoms.

Professor Abdullahi Idris discussed in details the manner and ways in which these colonial administrators of Nigeria deliberately balkanised the Nupe Empire and imposed a rather unfortunate kind of disunity on the Nupe Nation. By premeditated design they scattered the Nupe emirates and kingdoms in different localities whereby it will be difficult for these various Nupe emirates and kingdoms to unite into a single whole. Then they deliberately refused to build a bridge across the Niger to bring the Fulani and Tsudi dynasts of the Nupe kingdoms into such contact that will forge unity among them.

Now then, it should also be noted that the post-colonial authorities of Nigeria also by and large followed suite in perpetrating this unfortunate disunity among Nupencizhi. The First Republic authorities were, for instance, well aware of and lived in constant fear of the sociocultural might of the Nupe Nation and the threat posed to their administration by the possible renaissance of the Nupe Nation into a socio-political bulldozer in the Northern Region horizon. It was therefore quite convenient for the First Republic politicians to overlook the disunity of the Nupe Nation and to make no attempt at rectifying it.

So, there are varieties of disunity strands running through the fabrics of the Nupe society.

Edu State Will Unite Nupencizhi

But all these do not mean that Nupencizhi should not be brought to live together inside a Nupe commonwealth of Edu State. In fact, it is the bringing together of all Nupencizhi into such a commonwealth, wherein they all share a common stake in the geopolitical state, that will forge further unity among Nupencizhi. In other words, Edu State will unite Nupencizhi.

Those who claim that Nupencizhi are not united and therefore do not deserve a state of their own are being rather myopic in their reasoning.

We should take a cue from the case of the Federal Republic of Nigeria which is the result of a Colonial and foreign ideology of nation-statehood which was foisted on us by an alien British culture of old.

Emeka Esogbue wrote that, "The reason I feel indifferent to opinions that have arisen in condemnation of creation of more States in the Nigeria is that people who have been in condemnation of this arrangement fail to remember that the country is an artificial creation from many unrelated ethnic groups and tribes dissimilar in socially and religiously, and hurriedly put together for the benefit of the British."[1]

Now, had all these various Nigerian tribes and ethnicities not been forged into a Nigeria by the British colonialists, there is no way the sort of unity, however fragile, that is binding all the many Nigerian tribes and ethnicities (over 300 tribes) would have been possible.

The creation of Nigeria have united the diverse and formerly disunited people we call Nigerians today together. Emeka Esogbue added that, "The British tried to mould one geo-political entity with people that never imagined they could ever come together as one."[2]

Edu State will similarly unite all the diverse and different sections, classes and levels of the Nupe people into single whole.

---

[1] 'Creation of More States: Broad Way to Socio-economic Developments in Nigeria', by Emeka Esogbue, in Article Base

[2] 'Creation of More States: Broad Way to Socio-economic Developments in Nigeria', by Emeka Esogbue, in Article Base

Disunited Nupe Leaders

Some others also argue that our Nupe leaders are not united enough to effectively fight for the realisation of the dream of an Edu State.

I would like to state here that the unity of our Nupe leaders is not an absolute necessity for the creation of an Edu State.

As a matter of fact there is little, if any, unity among our Nupe leaders today. Our leaders and elders are seriously divided along religious, dialectal, cultural, and even geographical differences.

This heartrending disunity, however, does not preclude and cannot stop the realisation of the dream of statehood for the Nupe people. There are two main reasons for this. The first is the historical reason and the second is the generational reason.

Historical Reason

The historical reason has to do with the fact that human conduct and the course of human sociology is under the eternal laws of some historical factors that are unbending and, to a great extent, unexplainable to social scientists.

These historical laws and factors are today driving the Black race, Africa, Nigeria and the Nupe Nation forward even against our own wishes and mostly unknown to us. The point is that the workings of these historical factors are generally imperceptible to the unaided or to the cognition of the lay man. But the Nupe Nation is moving forward and is actually on the eve of a major historical development. The creation of a Nupe State in the immediate future is an inevitable part of this forthcoming monumental development.

So, it doesn't really matter whether our leaders are united or not - historical factors are moving us forward and our leaders and elders would only do themselves some good if they mend their differences and get united otherwise history will move the Nupe Nation along and leave them behind.

Generational Reason

The second reason, the generational reason, refers to the fact that though our Nupe leaders are not united the upcoming generation of younger Nupencizhi are united to a great extent. The religious, dialectal and cultural differences which our elders are brooding on have become completely irrelevant to the younger generation of Nupencizhi who would soon be the leaders and elders of the Nupe Nation.

The bottom line is that the younger generation are more united than the older generation because the younger generation have seen the absolute necessity of uniting together for the progress and development of the Nupe Nation.

But then, and to be fair to our elders and leaders, there is a sincere and genuine realisation on the part of our elders and leaders to get united today and they are actually taking steps to ensure that. As a matter of fact our leaders are more united today than they were, say, a couple of decades ago.

The Ethnic Make-up of Edu State

Many people have opposed the idea of a Edu State because they claim it is going to be an All-Nupe state in the very literal sense of the word. They argue that because Edu State is going to be composed of only Nupe people it will be more or less a tribal state in promotion of tribalism. And tribalism, they readily point out, is not proper.

One may not blame such people due to the fact that the very mention of or the very idea of Edu State almost always inevitably conjures up mental pictures of an All-Nupe state – a state wherein everybody is a Nupenci.

But the truth of the matter is that Edu State is not, and cannot, be a Nupe-only affair.

It is absolutely impossible to establish a state in Nigeria wherein all the citizens of the state are members of a single tribal or even ethnic group.

In a Nigeria wherein there are over three hundred ethnic groups, with an average of a tribal group to each three thousand square kilometres, it is absolutely impossible to have a single state constituted of only a single tribe or ethnic group.

Even a casual look at the projected map of Edu State will readily show us that it is comprised of sizeable sections of territories inhabited by people who are conventionally presumed to be non-Nupencizhi.

As a matter of fact the Learned Elders of Edu submitting the *Memorandum On the Request for the Creation of Edu State* to the Nigerian National Assembly, Abuja, categorically stated in the Memorandum that, "The proposed State consists of various tribal groups which include Nupe, Bisan, Gwari [Gbagyi], Dibo, Fulani, Kakanda, Hausa and Yoruba, united not only by geographical features but with a shared culture and history."[1]

Nobody, among the campaigners for the creation of Edu State, has ever thought of an Edu State comprised only of people of pure Nupe extractions. That of course would have been plain ethnocentrism or stark tribalism which is not characteristic of the true Nupe character. It is only the detractors of the Edu State Movement who kept on inventing the aspersion to the effect that the Edu State campaigners are campaigning for a 'Nupe only' state.

Even if the Edu State campaigners have thought of a 'Nupe only' state it would have still been practically impossible to create a state in Nigeria that is comprised of only members of a single tribe or a single ethnicity. The Edu State elders know better and that is why they categorically declared in the Edu State Memorandum that Edu State is going to be comprised of a diversity of tribes and ethnicities and not just Nupe alone.

---

[1] Section 2, article 4, Memorandum On the Request for the Creation of Edu State, p. 17.

In fact the projected map of Edu State is a composite jigsaw of a motley collection of tribes and ethnicities.

Non-Nupe Sections of Edu State

The northern parts of Edu State will be comprised of Gbagyi and Kambari settlements; the western tip of Edu State territories will be inhabited by the Gungawa and Bussawa people of the Borgu-Bussa emirate; the southern parts of Edu State will be comprised of people including the Yoruba, the Akoko or Kukuruku collection of tribes, the Igbomina, the Bassa Nge, Igbira, etc, etc; the eastern part of Edu State will be comprised of the Kakanda and a sundry other tribes to be found in today's FCT general area.

Edu State is a very heterogeneous entity. Edu State is going to be composed of various people including the Gbagyi of the Lapai general area; the Yoruba and Yagba of the Edu LGs of today's Kwara State; the Bassa, Kakanda, Igbira and others of today's Kogi State; the Bussawa and Gungawa of Borgu and New Bussa; the Dibo, the Kame, Gupa, even some Kambari and many other peoples you don't usually call Nupe.

All these people are going to be *bona fide* members of Edu State and will have and exercise the same state and citizenship rights as anybody else from Bida, Agaie, Lapai, Patigi or Lafiagi.

So, Edu State is going to be as heterogeneous as the Nigeria you talked about. That excruciating sameness many people dread in an 'All-Nupe Edu State' does not actually exist.

The Hausa Citizens of Edu State

Edu State is going to have a substantial and significant population of Hausa people. And these Hausa people will be *bona fide* and indigenous citizens of Edu State.

Right now you can see Hausa populations ubiquitously checkering the entire map of KinNupe. Wushishi and Zungeru are already parts of KinNupe overwhelmed by Hausa populations. Everywhere you go in KinNupe you see Hausa people settled as permanent indigenes - there is even a Umaru Sanda Sabon Gida Hausa settlement just a couple of kilometres out of Bida on the Bida Kataeregi road.

Well, nobody will or can chase these Hausa people out of Edu State because they are Nigerians and the Nigerian Constitution will not allow that.

Yoruba Citizens of Edu State

Edu State is also going to be comprised of a significant, and rather influential, population of Yoruba people.

Apart from the purely Yoruba settlements that will go into the formation of the southern fringes of the Edu State there are already teeming populations of Yoruba people intermixed within Nupe settlements in all parts of KinNupe.

The Yoruba people are a very enterprising people and for a very long time hardworking Yoruba migrant workers and petty traders have been migrating into every nook and corner of KinNupe. These enterprising Yoruba people have almost always ended up becoming acculturated into the local Nupe population. These Yoruba people are going to be part and parcel of the forthcoming Edu State and they are going to have the same, and equal, rights as the Nupe citizens of Edu State.

The Ibo Citizens of Edu State

The same story as we have just discussed above for the Yoruba people applies, to the last details, to the industrious Ibo people who have been migrating into KinNupe for a very long time now.

Other Citizens of Edu State

Furthermore, with the establishment of Edu State a lot of expatriates and migrant workers from different parts of the world and different parts of Nigeria will flood the capital cities of and will over the years become naturalised and acculturated as Educizhi.

The only thing Nupe about Edu State is the undeniable fact that Nupe is going to be the majority ethnicity in the state. And the Nupe language, after the English language of the Nigerian Constitution, will be the Official Language and the *Lingua Franca* of Edu State. But this does not mean that other minority ethnicities are going to be marginalised in Edu State.

As we have discussed over and over again, and according to the democratic spirit of the Nigerian Constitution, every citizen of Edu State, Nupe or non-Nupe, is going to have equal rights under the dictates of the Constitution of the Federal Republic of Nigeria.

The Constitutional Bottlenecks

Some others see the realisation of the dream of Edu State as impossible considering the fact that the constitutional requirements set at the National Assembly may be too numerous and too strict for the Ndaduma Prayers to effectively scale through.

Those who present constitutional logjams as the likely cause of the failure of the Edu State Cause are usually not completely opposed to the idea of an Edu State – they only feel that the entire Edu State enterprise is a waste of time and energy as it is most probably going to be frustrated by the constitutional stipulations set at the National Assembly.

And, to be realistic, the Constitutional stipulations set for the creation of a state at the National Assembly are quite high and rather strict.

The relevant State House of Assembly must first affirm that there is a genuine and realistic demand by a section of its people for the creation of a new state. Then the National Assembly must scrutinise and approve the given demand for the creation of the said state. Afterwards a referendum within the particular state must be conducted for the generality of the voters to approve the creation of the new state. Thereafter the state's House of Assembly must pass a referendum wherein at least two third of the seats approve the creation of the state.... and so on and so forth....

...These are, indeed, a terrifying collection of Constitutional bottlenecks that can discourage any unserious set of state creation agitators.

But these constitutional strictures, despite their discouraging demeanour, cannot and will not discourage the Edu State activists. If the authorities at Aso Rock will be impartial and adhere to the truth enough they will be able to see that the call for the creation of Edu State is a genuine and realistic one that can scale through the hurdles of constitutional scrutiny.

It was the Senate President, David Mark, who himself declared that, "We are not unmindful of the desire for state creation, we are going to be impartial and objective in consideration of the requests based on national interest and not on any sentiment. I believe in the truth, which will stand the test of time."[1]

Going by the avowed objectivity of the state creation exercise by the National Assembly, as stated by the Senate President above, there is no stopping the creation of Edu State from becoming a reality based on merit.

The reason is that the need for and the call for a Edu State is an overpowering one that is beyond the personal or individual power of the Edu State activist.

---

[1] David mark quoted in 'Constitution Review: Mark sets Conditions for State Creation', by Taiwo Adisa, in Nigerian Tribune, 11.06.2008.

Edu State and National Integration

Anti-Educizhi have argued that the creation of Edu State is another disintegrative step against the National Integration that the Constitution of the Federal Republic of Nigeria primarily stood for. These people claim that in the interest of National Integration the process of further state creation, including that of Edu State, should be stopped right away.

Those who are opposed to state creation for national integration reasons are doing so in a rather parochial manner.

These people also claim that the proliferation of state creation directly undermines the federal structure of the Nigerian system of government. Dr. Femi Mimiko, of Ondo State University, asserted that, "suffice it to say for now that creation of new States will not serve any useful purpose. Rather, it would further weaken the federal structure and keep Nigeria further away from the promised land of stability."[1]

They also say that the proliferation of states will lead to an over-dependence on the federal government which doles out federal allocations to the states on a monthly and annual basis.

---

[1] 'Before new States get created', by Dr. Femi Mimiko.

Back to the Regional System?

Some of these people have even gone to the extent of suggesting that not only should the process of state creation be immediately stopped but also that Nigeria should actually revert back to the three regional system of the pre-1963 era. They claim that ever since going beyond the stage of those three regions Nigeria has not made any tangible geopolitical progress.[1]

The Clement Ebri Presidential Constitution Review Panel went the extra, weird, step of even suggesting that further regions, and not states, should be created.

The glaring problem with all these call for the reversion to the regional system, whether three or more Regions, is the fact that it is more or less the same as the proliferation of states but with a different name and in a different administrative dimension. Whatever problems or troubles those opposed to the proliferation of states are afraid of they will eventually encounter in the reversion to or the proliferation of the regional system.

State Creation Will Not Undermine National Integration or Federalism

But the truth of the matter is that the proliferation of states within the Nigerian polity cannot weaken or destroy national integration or the federalism of the Nigerian overall state.

---

[1] 'Still On The Need For State Creation In Nigeria', by Emeka Esogbue, in Articles Base, Feb 25th, 2009.

The proliferation of states in Nigeria will, ironically enough, actually promote national integration. The simple reason is that the further the various Nigerian peoples are given their ethnic and tribal rights to statehood in the overall Nigerian polity the more all the various Nigerian peoples will feel as genuinely belonging to the Nigerian polity.

Professor Shehu Marafa categorically stated that it is the creation of Edu State that will give Nupencizhi a complete and total sense of belonging as far as Nigeria is concerned.[1]

It is on this note that Emeka Esogbue wrote that, "political grouping of peoples with similar linguistics, history, ancestries, traditions, and other criteria will guarantee sense of belonging..."[2]

It is only through the creation of more states that the complaints and plights those Nigerian ethnicities and tribes who feel marginalised can be adequately addressed in a consummate manner. The Learned Elders of Edu observed that "creating additional states would further remove a major source of political and social tensions, including fears of domination which had bred instability and frustration in various sections of the Federal Republic."[3]

The creation of more states will lead to the reduction in the inter-tribal and ethnic tensions and crises that the case in situations where different tribes and ethnicities are

---

[1] 'Nupe demand for Edu State', in VANGUARD, Friday, 03 October 2008.

[2] 'Creation of More States: Broad Way to Socio-economic Developments in Nigeria', by Emeka Esogbue, in Article Base

[3] Section 1, article 2, sub-section (iii), Memorandum on the Request for the Creation of Edu State, March 2009, p. 4.

incongruously combined and forced to live together in geopolitical states wherein one of the tribes is a majority while the other is a minority. Naturally the minority tribe feels marginalised while the majority tribe feels pestered or disturbed.

We can see that the state creation is a very effective tool for the reduction of tensions and crises in Nigeria. Even the history of state creation in Nigeria testifies to this fact. The first exercise of state creation by Gowon in the history of Nigeria was actually a step necessitated by the need to stop a major crises, the Biafran crises, that was then looming over the Nigerian horizon, from taking place. So, even the history of Nigeria shows that state creation is mainly an administrative exercise primarily designed to check or stem the proliferation of crises in Nigeria.

Even from this historical perspective we can see quite clearly that state creation is a tool designed for the prevention of crises in Nigeria. This is one thing most people are not aware of, namely, that the exercise of state creation is nothing more or less than a process addressed at stopping the proliferation of crises in Nigeria.

As a matter of fact an analytical study of the phenomenon of crises in Nigeria will readily reveal the fact that almost all the crises in Nigeria can be ultimately traced to grievances connected with the plight of those agitating for a geopolitical state of their own within the overall Nigerian polity. And this is regardless of whether the crisis under investigation masquerades under the guise of religious, ethnic or political crisis. Whatever form or guise any given crisis in Nigeria might assume the fact still remains that almost all crises in Nigeria can ultimately be traced back to an original grievance on the part of a people who are directly or indirectly agitating for a state of their own.

The recurrently perennial crises in Jos and Kaduna can, for instance, be readily traced to the direct or indirect agitation on the part of minority groups in these states for a state of their own. It is all about minority groups complaining that they are being unduly dominated and oppressed by majority groups. And, in fact, the Jos and Kaduna crises can readily be stopped or corrected by the creation of new states for the aggrieved minority groups.

The creation of a Kaduna South state will, for instance, readily bring an instant end to the so-called 'religious' crises that have perennially rocked Kaduna for a many years on end now. The same thing applies to the case of Jos. If only another state can be created for the aggrieved minority groups in Plateau State then the problem of the recurrent violent crises in Jos can be put to an end forever.

The same is the case with almost all the crises that have been taking place in all other parts of Nigeria. Most of the political crises that take place in Western Nigeria, in Yorubaland, for instance, can almost all be addressed through the creation of more states.

The Nigerian authorities should actually sit down and take a closer look at the untapped crises-shooting potentials of the exercise of state creation. The authorities will discover more and more that state creation will actually lead to a greater reduction in the number of crises in Nigeria.

The Nigerian authorities will readily see that almost all the hotspots of violence and crises on the Nigerian map are almost all places wherein are located minority groups that are agitating for a geopolitical state of their own. And if only these people can be given a state of their own then their grievances and the resultant crises will all come to an end. With a state of their own they will pipe down and stop all the crises they are fomenting.

The history of state creation in Nigeria actually substantiates the point we highlighted above. Take the case of all the people who were causing serious crises in the 1960s and '70s so instance; all of them have stopped fomenting crises today because they have states of their own. Usually such crises arise from people who felt that they are being dominated or oppressed in the state they share with other, usually, dominant or majority groups. And if only such people could be given a state of their own then such fears will be put to an end.

We should note that this same problem is what applies to the Nupe people today. This is particularly the case with Nupencizhi who are living as minority groups in states other than Niger State. In states like Kwara and Kogi we can see very well that the Nupe people in these states are seriously aggrieved because they felt dominated and oppressed by the dominant tribes and ethnicities in their respective states.

The plight and grievance of the Nupencizhi in Kwara, Kogi and other states where we are a minority is a constant source of serious crises that often masquerades under religious, political and atimes even openly ethnic crises and violence.

The same scenario of the Nupe people in Kwara State applies to the Nupe people of Kogi State who are also minority tribal or ethnic groups in a Kogi State dominated by other tribes that are the majority. All the various Nupe people of Kogi State — including the Dibo, the Kakanda, Bassa Nge, and others — felt that they are being dominated and unduly oppressed by the Igbira, the Igala and other majority tribes of Kogi State. All these Nupe people in Kogi State are aggrieved and, once in a while, do resort to open or indirect violence in voicing out their complaints.

The only way to address and stop these inter-tribal and inter-ethnic clashes and crises between Nupe minorities in Kwara, Kogi and other states with the majority tribal or ethnic groups in these various states is through the creation of Edu State wherein all these various Nupe people from different states can be brought together to live in an All-Nupe geopolitical state.

Then we also need to clarify the fact that even in Niger State, where Nupencizhi claim to be the majority, there is this perpetual tension between Nupencizhi and other, minority, ethnic peoples in Niger State.

Now we can see that the only way to address these crises in all these states where Nupencizhi are either minorities or majorities is by creating a state for the Nupe people – a geopolitical state of their own in the form of Edu State. A Nupe State where all the Nupe people can live together and nobody can then claim or alleged to be dominated or oppressed by a non-Nupe tribe or ethnicity. Edu State is the only solution to this problem of inter-tribal and inter-ethnic tension and crises between Nupencizhi and non-Nupencizhi that is now overwhelming Nupencizhi wherever they live either as minority or majority tribe or ethnic group.

I think if we take it from that angle we are going to see that state creation is the best way of addressing all the different types of crises in Nigeria.

International Instances

Those who are opposed to the idea of the proliferation of states in the Nigerian federation are not aware of the fact that the proliferation of states and local governments in other countries has actually promoted national integration in various countries in several parts of the world.

I will categorically cite the example of the proliferation of local governments in the British polity. The large number of local governments in the British polity has actually led to the further national integration of the United Kingdom as a whole.

State Creation Promotes Federalism

The proliferation of states in the Nigerian polity will actually go to strengthen the federal structure of Nigeria further. That is what those campaigning against the creation of further states in Nigeria are not aware of. But our discussions and demonstrations so far have categorically shown that the exercise of state creation actually strengthens the Nigerian federal system.

The Learned Elders of Edu are well aware of this fact when they stated in the Edu State Memorandum that "the creation of more states is a necessary requirement for achieving a much more balanced and stable federation."[1]

As a matter of fact the call for the Creation of Edu State is a call for a promotion of the Nigerian federation.

State Creation Promotes Democracy

Anti-Educizhi campaigning against the proliferation of states in the Nigerian polity are also unaware of the fact that state creation and proliferation are exercises in promotion of democracy in Nigeria. Uchenna Okereke observed that, "There is no doubt the huge number of demands for states derives from the prevailing democratic climate in the country."[2]

---

[1] Section 1, article 2, sub-section (i), Memorandum on the Request for the Creation of Edu State, March 2009, p. 3.

[2] 'Nigeria: Jaded By The Politics Of State Creation?', by Uchenna Okereke, in The Nigerian Village Square, Friday, 07 November 2008.

The point is that the further the number of states the more the entrenchment of democratic values in the administrative and geopolitical makeup of the Nigerian polity. It is in this context that the Learned Elders of Edu observed that, "the creation of more states would further extend and spread the democratisation process and decentralisation of power."[1]

The creation of more states is an exercise in promotion of democracy. I don't think anybody can actually deny this fact. Democracy has to do with extending power to the people; bringing power down to the level of the people at the grassroots. And, of course, the more states we create the more power we give to the people. And as we can see state creation is actually more or less a way of extending power down to the level of the people – exactly what democracy is all about. So, the creation of more states is an exercise in promotion of democracy. The creation of Edu State is, accordingly, an exercise in promotion of democracy.

If we have a state wherein a majority tribe and a minority tribe are locked in a power-struggle whereby the minority tribes complains of marginalisation while the majority tribe complains of insecurity, the easiest and most democratic solution that state of affairs is the creation of a state for the minority tribe in order to stem the tide of the complaints from both the minority and majority tribes in the former state. By

---

[1] Section 1, article 2, subsection (ii), Memorandum on the Request for the Creation of Edu State, March, 2009, p. 4.

so doing the democratic rights of both the minority and majority tribes, are being addressed.

We should also note the fact that the creation of a state leads to the inevitable creation of more local governments and wards which is an indubitable way of bringing government down to the level of the masses at the grassroots, the ultimate goal of democracy. So, state creation is a democratic process that cannot be separate one from the other.

State creation is also an effective means of decentralising power from the federal to the grassroots levels. Through the decentralisation of power at the federal level power is brought closer to the people at the grassroots level; exactly what democracy is all about. This is the democratisation of power.

The decentralisation of power through the creation of state also comes in the form of divesting a part of the power reposed in the hands of a majority or hegemonist tribe and giving it to a minority tribe to whom the new state have been accorded. The creation of a state decentralises power from the hands of the majority to the hands of the minority tribes. In this way the majority tribe is prevented from wrongfully dominating the minority tribe and also from wrongfully holding the federal government to ransom due to the extra or excessive geopolitical powers in its, the majority tribe's, possession.

As a matter of fact this is another aspect of the decentralisation of power that is often overlooked by most people, namely, that the more power reposed in the hands of majority tribes or ethnic groups the more undue influence such majority tribe or ethnicity exercises on the federal government – a totally undemocratic or even anti-democratic phenomenon. And it is only through the creation of more states for minority groups that the balance of power and the exertion of such power on the federal government can be even out such that one tribe doesn't have undue advantage over the other at the federal level.

The fewer the number of states the more the power of the majority tribes and hegemonist ethnicities at the federal level because an overwhelming majority of the available states will be dominated by these majority tribes. But the more the number of states the more the number of minority tribes and ethnicities that would have been freed from bondage in states with the majority tribes and the more these minority tribes will be represented at the federal level because they now have a geopolitical state of their own. This is a democratic way of offsetting the undue power of the majority tribes at the federal level.

Why Edu State Will Not Fail Again

The question may be asked as to why all previous attempts at the creation of Edu State have failed and why are we so confident that this time around it will not fail once more?

The first question may be answered with the simple fact that we Nupe people have failed to actualise our eternal dream at the creation of Edu State mainly because we are not the paramount power brokers in Nigeria.

We have never been able to produce a president, a vice president or a superpower statesman in the likes of Sir Ahmadu Bello the Sardauna of Sokoto, Chief Awolowo, General Babangida, Chief Obasanjo, General Atiku, or the likes.

And because it is all a vicious cycle sort of thing, our lack of real power at Aso Rock is self-perpetuating in that it contributes to our inability to influence things in favour of the creation of Edu State at Aso Rock which further undermines our power-brokering ability at Aso Rock.

The only way to break out of this vicious dilemma is to take the bull by the horns and let it gore its way to satiety — after all we should know that achieving the creation of Edu State is not going to be without its own sacrifices.

We are not powerful enough at the National Assembly or at Aso Rock in particular simply because we have been taking things for granted in a laisser-faire manner for so long. Now is the time to really buckle up and struggle for our right to a State, Edu State, in Nigeria.

In the past the struggle for Edu State has been in the form an abstract or rhetorical form that did not involve actual physical activism on a sustained level. This is the main reason why the struggle for Edu State has failed in the past.

Now we have to go beyond the rhetorical into the practical aspect of the struggle for the creation of Edu State. We have to go beyond the theoretical into the pragmatic aspect of the Edu State Movement.

This generation is not the first to demand for the creation of Edu State.

As a matter of fact Professor Shehu Marafa Bida publicly declared that the Edu State Movement has been on for at least twenty years. Well, Alhaji Egba Enagi once told me that they have been involved in the Edu State struggle since before the creation of Niger State, that is over forty years ago!

We are simply the latest generation of Nupencizhi who will not overlook our fundamental right to having our own geopolitical State in the heart of our beloved Nigeria.

Edu State is a Popular Cause

The Nigerian authorities at Aso Rock maintain that the creation of any new state in Nigeria must, first and foremost, be based on popular demand by the people of the proposed state. Senator David Mark, the Senate President, will always insist that it must be based on merit.

Uchenna Okereke, in this regard, wrote that, "Before any demand for a state appears on the national stage, it must be seen to have been clamoured for by the masses and not a creation of a single or a few political weight lifters who rent a crowd and head to the National Assembly to demand for a new state as we see some evolving lately; otherwise the issue of state creation becomes a very big distraction and extra burden for the relevant organs of government."[1]

In this context of a popular demand, the call for the creation of Edu State is a very successful one.

A major reason why the creation of the Edu State is inevitable is the fact that the call for a Edu State is a popular one. There is hardly any other call for the creation of a state in the history of state creation in Nigeria that has enjoyed the overwhelming popular support of the masses as has the call for the creation of Edu State.

Throughout the length and breadth of KinNupe the voice of the masses is a deafening one in popular support of the creation a Edu State. The Nigerian authorities at the Three Arms Zone, Aso Rock, who kept on hankering at the absolute condition of a popular support before they can ratify the creation of a given state will be flabbergasted by the overwhelming popular support that the call for the creation of Edu State enjoys at the grassroots level right across the length and breadth of KinNupe.

---

[1] Nigeria: Jaded By The Politics Of State Creation?', by Uchenna Okereke, in The Nigerian Village Square, Friday, 07 November 2008.

In the case of the call for the creation of new states in various quarters of Nigeria state creation has been more or less an elitist affair used by the elites to indulge their selfish or narrow-minded interests. It is in this regard that Dr. Femi Mimiko wrote that, "devoid of all its facades, State creation in Nigeria remains an entirely elite affair. It is an enterprise contorted, prosecuted and employed by the elite for the satisfaction of elite desire for power and relevance and all the appurtenances that go with that."[1]

The elites have found in the exercise of state creation a potent weapon for the promotion of their selfish interests. Abubakar Sadeeque Abba noted that, "The basic language these elites understand is how to further their nest of corruption, political prostitution, business empires and poverty among the people. They evolve all kind of strategies including the doctrine of state creation to achieve their objectives."[2]

The elitist manipulation of state creation as a weapon of personal political and administrative aggrandisement has led given the exercise of state creation all the bad and negative stigma that it is characterised with today. Dr. Femi Mimiko rightly added that, "This is why even 38 years after the first State (Region) was created in 1963, the phenomenon has not been a basis for resolving the national question and the attendant problem of mass alienation from the political and

---

[1] 'Before new States get created', by Dr. Femi Mimiko.
[2] 'After the agitation what next?', by Abubakar Sadeeque Abba, in Newspage Weekly

economic processes of the nation, which it supposedly set out to do in 1963."[1]

But, interestingly enough, the elite have expressed little, if any serious interest, in the creation of Edu State. The call for the creation of Edu State has, all along, mainly been a popular call by the masses.

Unlike in the politicised and personalised cases of many other calls for the creation of states in other parts of Nigeria, in the case of the call for the creation of Edu State the masses seem to be more serious than the elite.

It is rather evident that a major section of the Nupe elite is generally lackadaisical concerning the call for the creation of Edu State. Majority of the leaders of the Nupe Nation generally exhibit a lukewarm attitude towards the question of the creation a Edu State mainly because the masters, non-Nupe masters, they serve are not in support of the creation of a Nupe State.

On the other hand the overwhelming generality of the Nupe masses, who serve no any non-Nupe master, are the ones rallying a juggernaut of a popular support for the call for the creation of a Edu State.

The creation of Edu State is an inevitable event that must come to past, God willing, for the singular reason that it is a popular demand on the part of the Nupe populace – it is the unstoppable voice of the masses.

---

[1] 'Before new States get created', by Dr. Femi Mimiko.

The Population Power of Nupe

Another formidable factor in pointing to the inevitability of the Edu State is the overwhelming population power of the Nupe Nation.

In the entire region of the Nigerian Middle Belt the Nupe Nation is the most densely populated. That is apart from the fact that the Nupe Nation has the largest population of all the various peoples of the Nigerian Middle Belt.

But then, even outside the Middle Belt, the population of the Nupe Nation is a surpassing one.

Unknown to most people, and even to the generality of the Nupencizhi themselves, the population of the Nupe Nation is the largest of all ethnic and tribal groups in Nigeria.

And, whether, we know it or not, this population supremacy of the Nupe Nation will one day become an unstoppable weapon in the fight for the imperative creation of an Edu State.

In my book titled *Nupe the Fourth Force* I persuasively but grippingly prove the fact that Nupe is the largest tribe or ethnic group in Nigeria today.

Forget the colonial and post-colonial hegemonist conspiracies of rating the Hausa, Yoruba and Ibo as the largest ethnic groups in Nigeria; all that scrap is a spurn of pure lies.

In the book *Nupe the Fourth Force* I arrayed irrefutable demographic, linguistic and statistical evidences in prove of the fact that the true population of Nupencizhi today is more than that of the Hausa, Fulani, Yoruba or Ibo.